Educator's Treasury of Humor
For All Occasions

Also by William R. Gerler

Executive's Treasury of Humor for Every Occasion

Educator's Treasury of Humor
For All Occasions

WILLIAM R. GERLER

Parker Publishing Company, *West Nyack, N.Y.*

Library of Congress Cataloging in Publication Data

Gerler, William R   comp.
    Educator's treasury of humor for all occasions.

    1. Teaching--Anecdotes, facetiae, satire, etc.
I. Title.
LA23.G4   371.1'02'0207   72-5871
ISBN: 0-13-240762-0

Dedicated to:

My Father, William C. Gerler, a
grand octogenarian who has loved
humor all his life.

HUMOR AND ITS PLACE IN EDUCATION

Educators who rely largely on speech for their livelihood recognize the many benefits of humor in speech, and become proficient in the use of techniques for selecting, personalizing and adapting humor properly for a variety of situations.

Humor is a fundamental ingredient in both formal and informal speaking. It adds savor to speech just as a culinary spice flavors and improves a cooking dish. And like a spice, humor must be selected with care, used in the right proportion and added at the right time. Properly used, humor makes any formal or informal speech more palatable to the listener. It also helps to make tense situations more comfortable and dull gatherings more bearable.

Educators who use humor in their classroom are more likable and better accepted by all with whom they work, teach and associate. Humor is the one great elixir of life and there is no better place to practice it than in actual teaching.

For educators, humor is used best when it serves a definite purpose and not solely for entertainment. It can help make a subject clearer, remembered longer. It can cut through some of the fog of a difficult subject and turn students "on."

Elaine G. Denholtz, instructor at Fairleigh Dickinson University, writing in "Today's Education," has this advice: "Every teacher, whether he teaches sixth grade chorus or a graduate seminar in Advanced Comparative Anatomy of the Vertebrates—wants to get to his students to make them care about the subject, to engender excitement and involvement. I try to turn my students on by preparing for a performance each time we meet. Before class, I consider the theme (of the lesson, lecture, discussion), the costumes, the scenery, the pacing, the setting, the plot, the dramatic effects, the music, the lighting—the entire production," she commented.

"A teacher sells himself first. Of course, he must be competent, knowledgeable, scholarly. That's content. But what about his performance? Does he understand timing, or does he spit out information at an unvarying rate like a teletypewriter? Is his voice dull and unchanging in pitch and volume? Can he make his students laugh, make them angry, make them argue, make them find out?"

HUMOR IS A NECESSITY IN EDUCATION

You don't have to be a comedian or a natural wit to use humor as an educator. Most likely you aren't. Sam Levenson, the noted professional humorist, is the exception. He loved humor so much that he made it a full-time career after serving many years as an educator. They say he got his start by trying out jokes on his students.

In commenting on humor for educators especially for this book, he said: "I have been a practitioner of humor in the classroom and consider it not a luxury, but an absolute necessity. Viva laughter!"

THE SECRET OF EFFECTIVE HUMOR

Basically, there are two types of humor that are being practiced today. One is the type that relies on the element of "surprise" or "shock." This is the type that has a surprise ending, or punch line as it is called. You usually can't foresee the climax of this type of humor.

> "What position do you play on the basketball team?" a teacher asked her student.
> "Oh, sort of crouched and bent over," he replied.

The other type of humor is just the opposite where the punch line of a familiar joke is slowly leaked so that the listener is smiling even before it is finished.

8

TYPES OF HUMOR AND HOW TO USE THEM

Years ago educators would spend 20 minutes or more developing a humorous sketch and their audience loved it. Not so today. The humor that is most popular today is the short, brief joke that quickly illustrates a point. Many call it the "witticism." It's the type of humor heard most frequently on television and practiced by such well-known humorists as Bob Hope, Flip Wilson, Johnny Carson, Phyllis Diller and others.

You will find many examples of good witticisms in this book. The witticism takes advantage of situations and transfers them into humor. They're fast, sharp . . . and when properly used, the most effective of today's humor.

> A teacher looks over his students in a very noisy classroom.
> "I'll not begin today's lecture until this room settles down," he says.
> A student in the back of the room shouts, "Why don't you go home and sleep it off."
> That's a witticism—short, startling, even clever. It may even be rude as in this example, but you will find that it is very popular and widely accepted.

The "humorous story" is the type of humor that is memorized in advance and used for a specific purpose such as an introduction or to illustrate some subject. It is longer than the witticism and builds up slowly to the punch line.

TIPS ON USING HUMOR

Try to avoid jokes about religion, nationalities, politics or personal characteristics *unless* you know your audience well enough to be sure that they will not be offended. These jokes are usually reserved for intimate personal groups of friends and seldom have a place in the classroom.

Also, don't use regional humor unless the humor applies to the particular audience of the locality in which the joke is being told. An out-of-town group would enjoy a joke about their own home town, but generally jokes about Los Angeles smog fall flat in Iowa. New York and Chicago traffic jokes don't go over in Spring Green, Wisconsin.

If you want to use regional humor use local situations. Most towns have their own jokes that can be used for a sure laugh with those who can appreciate them.

Another suggestion is to practice telling jokes and practice using humor. There's nothing more ineffective than telling a joke and then muffing the punch line. Recite jokes to yourself driving alone or when you are alone in your home or apartment. Tell them to other people if they will listen to you. The more you practice a joke, the more effective it becomes. The timing is better. Your inflections are better. Your own personality comes through.

Also, memorize jokes and stories you, yourself, like best. We all have our favorite type of humor and it is the easiest to tell.

It's also better to personalize a joke with a name and a place that fits the situation. Use names that people know or members of your own faculty, relatives and family. Instead of telling a story about some student, use a name of your own son or daughter.

"My brother-in-law embarrassed us at the school banquet the other night. He drank his soup and six couples got up and danced."

Instead of saying: "Many a house has been 'bugged' by miniature snooping devices for several years. They repeat every word all over school."

Say: "Our house has been 'bugged' by a miniature snooping device for several years. Our daughter, Laurie, repeats every word at Emerson School."

While this book contains a unique collection of miscellaneous short jokes, stories, poems, ancedotes, witticisms, epigrams, quotations, definitions and other types of humorous treasures, I suggest that you add to this collection yourself with humor that you personally hear and read. Wise teachers keep their own collections for occasions such as those described in the following chapter. Today's channels of communications are storehouses of material of which this book should be only the start.

William R. Gerler

ACKNOWLEDGMENTS

While this collection of humor has been compiled from a great number of sources, I particularly want to acknowledge D.R. McCleary, formerly of the Genuine Parts Company who has granted permission to use jokes and witticisms from the very amusing publication, *Parts Pups,* which he created and edited for many decades; Department Editor Mary T. Steyn, *Readers' Digest;* James A.C. Thom, editor of *Nuggets;* Robert Duckett, Vice Principal, Waukesha, Wisc., High School (South Campus); Kenneth E. Gerler; and Barbara Gerler Sorensen, my daughter and former art instructor, who devoted many hours during a summer vacation to type the manuscript for this book.

Other publications from which material in this book was extracted include *Smiles, Grit, Journeyman Barber, Canadian Farm Equipment Dealer, Advertisers' Digest, Master Barber and Beautician, Drug Topics, Great Northern Goat, L & N Magazine, Future Farmer, Christian Science Monitor, This Week, Pit and Quarry, Georgia Grocer, Cavalier, Barbs, Family Weekly, Oklahoma Farm Journal, Sales Meetings, Wall Street Journal,* "Today's Chuckle," and the *Milwaukee Journal.*

CONTENTS

Part One

HOW TO USE
THIS BOOK FOR
SPECIFIC SITUATIONS

Humor can be used in many ways by educators. It can be used successfully to capture the attention of students at an assembly or to enliven a roomful of parents at a P.T.A. meeting. It is useful at a teachers' conference, at an alumni meeting and a graduation ceremony.

It can be helpful at almost any meeting in which you take part whether you are presiding or a participant. It can be used at school functions as well as outside meetings in the community with parents or civic groups.

Coaches of athletic teams can use humor to help change the mood of their athletes during competition or in training. And at social situations, humor is valuable in making social introductions or in putting some fun into what could be a dull gathering.

This book contains many valuable quotes and stories that make it particularly useful in the classroom to inspire and to make a dull subject more interesting.

How does one go about using this book for specific situations? What are some of the situations where humor can be used successfully and how will this book help?

Here are a few situations where humor can be used for educators.

PTA MEETING

Getting a P.T.A. meeting off to a good start is often accomplished by some personal humorous anecdote or you can use one or more of the jokes found in this book, particularly under the classification of students, children, teachers, parents, kindergarten, school, education, discipline, family life, homework and other categories.

You could use this example:

> My second graders were talking about the different combinations of coins that give a total of 10 cents. One girl said that two nickels make 10 cents. Another added that one dime makes 10 cents. A third volunteered that one nickel and five pennies made 10 cents and a girl added that 10 pennies also makes 10 cents.
>
> I felt that the children had exhausted all possibilities until one

17

boy in the back of the room raised his hand. He said that he had another combination that made 10 cents. When I asked what it was he said, "Two big pop bottles also make 10 cents."

You will also get a laugh if you tell the story at a P.T.A. meeting about the mother of one of the students who was asked by a neighbor how her children were doing in school.

"Better," she replied, "but I still go to P.T.A. meetings under an assumed name."

TEACHERS' CONFERENCE

Teachers appreciate humor that portrays their own problems. The classification "Teachers" has some outstanding examples of humor that can be used effectively when you are participating at a teachers' conference. Here's one example that could get such a meeting off to a good start:

"Some years back," you say, "I taught school in a community that had 54 drop-outs within the first three weeks. That's right, 54. And do you know what? Fifty-two of them were teachers."

Or you could select this one:

I had an interesting experience the other day with one of those parents who are always trying to have us give their kids special consideration. I believe they're now learning things from the psychologists. I had a talk with one of them, for example, about her son's bad behavior and asked her what she thought I ought to do about it.

"Hit the boy next to him," she said, "and that will frighten Melvin."

ALUMNI MEETING

Almost annually, teachers are asked to participate in one or more alumni meetings of the various classes of their school. This calls for a number of humorous stories and you'll find a collection of them in the sections on "Alumni," "Graduation" or "Parents."

One particularly good story for these groups is the following:

I was talking with two of our alumni a short time ago who met for the first time since they graduated from General High. One had been an excellent student at the very top of his class. The other had a tough time getting through. The latter, however, seemed to have prospered in the business world.

"Joe," I said. "You seem to have done exceptionally well since you left General High. How did you do it?"

"Well," he said. "After graduation I found that I wasn't so bright, and didn't feel I could get through college, so I found a product I could make for one dollar and sell for five dollars. Believe me, that steady 400 per cent really added up over the years."

INTRODUCTIONS

One of the many opportunities for educators is to introduce people at various functions and to serve as toastmaster on various occasions.

When planning an introduction, find out as many things as you can about the person you plan to introduce—his education, his schools, his family life, his hobbies, his achievements and other personal information that will help you select the most appropriate story. Then select a joke from this book that matches the person. The situation, of course, need not be true, but it should be humorous.

For example, you have been asked to serve as a toastmaster at a luncheon to introduce a new principal of your school. You select a story about a married man and tell this one to introduce him:

> Our new principal, before this luncheon, was telling me that he has the answer to the perfect marriage. After being married 15 years, he and his wife, Mary, still set aside two nights a week for dining out. They go for soft music, thick steaks and all the extras that make up a "night out" dinner.
>
> I told him that I thought it wonderful for married people to do that, but I asked him if it wasn't costing a fortune for baby sitters.
>
> "Oh, no," he replied. "Mary baby sits with the children when I go out for dinner on Tuesday nights and I keep them when she's out for dinner on Thursday nights."

SCHOOL ASSEMBLY

School assemblies call for a great deal of different types of humor to gain attention of the students, to inspire them, to enlist their support of school-sponsored activities.

You may be enlisting support for school activities and tell this humorous story found in the "Students" classification:

> There's a great deal of talk about apathy in our school. So 1000 students were asked if they were apathetic. Forty-four said "Yes," sixty-nine said "No," and 887 had no opinion.

You could be promoting the new class play and tell this experience:

> "The first day of school, I asked my students in our literature class who Shakespeare was. One student raised his hand and when I asked him "who?" he said, "He's the guy who writes all the school plays."

You may be discussing leadership and look under the classification "Leadership" for the following:

> Leadership in teaching is the art of getting somebody else to learn something you want him to learn because he wants to learn it.

SPORTS RALLY

Finding good humor for a Sports Rally is not easy, but you will probably enjoy this one from the classification "Sports":

> The Russians have produced outstanding athletes in recent years, particularly in the field events. They have won many Olympic honors and have set new records in recent decades.
>
> I have often wondered how they do this, so I asked an American sportswriter why it is that the Soviets produce such fast runners.
>
> "It's quite simple," he said. "In their starting guns they use *real* bullets."

Or this one:

I had a football player in my class last year who always rushed into class ten minutes late.

I wondered about this until I overheard him say to another classmate, "I hate to be late for Professor Smith's class all the time, but you know I really need the sleep.

Another good rally story, particularly at a football rally:

We're in the short week period of the year now—Monday, Tuesday, Wednesday, Thursday, Football, Football, Football.

INSPIRATION MEETINGS

There are many opportunities for teachers to address student groups that are primarily to inspire them. In the classifications, "Life," "Success," and "Leadership" are excellent stories for this. You might select this one from the "Life" section:

George Washington Carver, the Negro botanist, chemist and educator (1864-1943) whose research developed profitable uses of such humble crops as the peanut and the soybean, often summarized his life philosophy with this story:

"When I was young I said to God, 'God, tell me the mystery of the universe.' "

"But God answered, 'That knowledge is reserved for Me alone.' "

"So I said, 'God, tell me the mystery of the peanut.' "

"Then God said, 'Well, George, that's more nearly your size.' And He told me."

That for some reason, seems to us to be one of the greatest little stories ever told. It's a peanut-sized story, but it has universe-sized meanings in it. Like the saying about the great oak growing from the tiny acorn, it seems to be an illustration of the way greatness is related to humility.

Another from the same classification:

One student gets nothing but discord out of a piano; another harmony. No one claims the piano is at fault. Life is about the same. The discord is there; the harmony is there. Study to play it correctly and it will give forth beauty. Play it falsely and it will give forth ugliness.

STAFF MEETINGS

Frequently staff meetings of teachers need a little humor to make them more interesting.

This is the opportunity to have fun with some of the common peeves of teachers and the entire school system. You might use the following from the classification "School Bus," but there are many others in the classification, "Teachers," "School," "Education," "College," "Tradition," "High School," "Kindergarten," "School Board," or any of the specific types of education.

> The other day I was watching an ironworker nonchalantly walking a beam about 30 stories above the ground.
> When he came down, I couldn't help but walk over to him and say, "I was amazed by your calmness up there. How did you happen to go to work on a job like this?"
> "Well," he said, "I used to drive a school bus but my nerves gave out." Or you could change this to "I used to be a school teacher, but my nerves gave out."

Another for such a meeting:

> I just heard that in the Lake County School District the Board of Trustees is trying to stop necking. Isn't that something? The first thing you know they'll be trying to make teachers and students stop, too.

This may also be good for a laugh in a large school or university staff meeting:

> You know, I really feel sorry for the kids going to school nowadays. Lots of them have to walk nearly as far to their parked cars as we used to walk from our homes to school.

SERVICE CLUBS

Frequently teachers are invited to address local service clubs or other community groups on subjects relating to education. These appearances call for some humor and you might find humor that makes some fun out of education useful for a meeting such as these.

If you are a supervisor of a school district, you could use this story:

> When a teacher's legs give out, they make him a department head. When a department head's brains give out, they make him a supervisor.

These under "Parenthood," could be useful in a meeting in the community:

> A father once confessed to me of the problems of parenthood by saying that his oldest son is in college and his youngest in nursery school. "Sometimes," he said, "you can hardly tell the difference."
>
> Any parent will confirm that youngsters are at their mental peaks at age 4 and age 17. At 4 they know all the questions. At age 17 they know all the answers.
>
> The two most difficult careers in life that are trusted to amateurs are Citizenship and Parenthood. Sometimes the teaching profession feels the same way.
>
> I talked with a father of one of my students recently who said that he had said to his son: "When I went to school, I walked five miles a day."
> His son replied, "And what were you protesting, Dad?"

If you are talking to a woman's group, you might use this joke that pertains to the "Liberation Movement":

> Today we are concerned with the liberation movement for women. Actually, the biggest breakthrough in women's liberation takes place when schools open in the fall.

LUNCHROOM CONVERSATION

There's always an opportunity for teachers to spread a little humor at lunch with other teachers. You may have a number of anecdotes to recite as a result of your personal activities of the day. These are the most acceptable and are preferred over other humor. Should you lack a good personal experience, some of these might be appropriate:

Before the lunch program was started, I took my first grade class to the lunch room to explain the procedure. I assigned tables, explained how to carry the tray and how to behave. As we returned to our classrooms, I overheard one of the students remark, "What a dumb teacher. She forgot to let us eat."

You could also select this experience from the section on "Children":

I asked my students today if they could take their warm overcoats off and received an affirmative reply from all of them.

Then I asked them if the bear could take off his warm overcoat.

"No, Ma'm," was the reply from one of the students.

"Why not?" I asked.

After a long silence he said, "only God knows where the buttons are."

One of my children today asked me where elephants come from. "And don't give me that routine of the stork. I know better."

COMMUNITY MEETINGS

Teachers and administrators are frequently asked to participate in various types of community activities where they are asked to talk on aspects of education. This is the opportunity to relate education to the family life. Stories such as these often have a favorable response from the local audience:

I have found that sending a youngster through college these days is very educational. It teaches his parents how to do without a lot of things.

One of my neighbors stopped me the other day and stated that his son is now in college. "How is he making it?" I asked him.

"He's not," he replied.

"Oh?" I answered with surprise. I knew he was a good student.

"That's right," he said, "I'm the one that's making it. He's spending it."

Another . . . For a teacher of first grade students:

A funny thing happened this morning right after the opening

of school. A pair of first grade students approached me after the first day of class and asked me, "What does G-I-R-L-S spell?"

"Why, girls," I said.

One of them looked at the other and said, "I told you we were in the wrong room!"

A general story for all teachers:

In our faculty cloakroom we have a sign that says, "For faculty members only."

Above the row of hooks, someone wrote "May also be used for hats and coats."

GRADUATION CEREMONIES

Graduation ceremonies can demand both humor and inspirational messages. You will find both types of reference material in this book.

For humor you might be able to use this quip that is found in the section "Graduation":

Now is the time when all of you graduates learn that you can't get rich by degrees.

Or another from the same section:

I overheard one father say to another as he was entering this room. "I was photographing my son a short time ago and told him that he would look more natural if he stood with his hand out!"

In the section on college are some appropriate stories for high school graduations, such as this—

Many of you will be entering college next fall and will be leaving (name of town) for some college or university campus in another city. I hope that you will appreciate your college years because it is the only vacation a boy gets between his mother and his wife.

One commencement speaker told his graduation class of men:

To keep up your education, sit down and read whenever your

25

wife tells you she is ready to go out except for her hat and gloves. You'll be amazed how much knowledge you'll acquire that way.

FRESHMAN INDOCTRINATION

Getting a new class of high school or college freshmen properly indoctrinated and helping them feel at home in their new environment is frequently aided by some humorous stories or anecdotes. The following are suggestions:

> One of our freshman girls told me today that she had written to 65 colleges for admission and finally picked (name of your school) because it had the highest rating. She said she was told that we had in the freshman class last year 1,240 boys and 365 girls.

Or another:

> I don't believe that many of you know that public schools such as ours have rules against dispensing any kind of medication, even aspirin. We have the right to give you a headache, but not to give you anything to cure it.

> Some of you may be planning to take advanced degrees when you receive your bachelor's degree. We believe that to be admirable, but I hope that you won't be like the son of one father who was asked what his son was going to be when he finished his education and replied, "an octogenarian!"

TEACHERS' LOUNGE

Relating experiences in classes is one of the pleasures of conversing with teachers in the lounge. It also offers some such as these:

> You will discover that in nearly every class there is a youngster eager to argue. Your first impulse will be to silence him but I advise you to think carefully before doing so. He probably is the only one listening.

> You heard about the English teacher who regarded Santa's helpers as a bunch of subordinate clauses.

> One of the teachers in my former school graded so hard that she even took off for upside-down periods.

Boy is that principal at (other school) strict. He told one of the new teachers that if he let him take two hours off for lunch and find a substitute for his class he would have to do the same for every other teacher whose wife gave birth to quadruplets.

It's hard for any student to realize that in another 20 years, he will be as dumb as his parents are now.

Not only is he the worst behaved child in my class but he also has the best attendance record.

CLASSROOM

This book has been created primarily for the everyday use by many different educators in their day-to-day activities with students, principally in their classrooms. The humor collected will make the subject clearer, remembered longer and help teachers establish a better rapport with their students.

Here are typical examples how teachers can use the humor in this book for specific classroom activities.

GENERAL

There are many excellent examples of humor scattered throughout this book under the general subjects of "Education," "Students," "Teachers," "Schools," "High School," "College" and other general classifications that have material that can be used by all teachers. In the section on education, you could use:

Minds are like parachutes. They only function when they are open.

A good deal of education is like the Indian Snake Dance. It seldom brings rain, but it makes the dancer feel better.

Learn by the mistakes of others. You can't live long enough to make them all yourself.

The human body is extremely sensitive. Pat a student on the back and his head swells.

An intelligence test sometimes shows a man how smart he'd have been not to have taken it.

School is the mouse race that equips you for the rat race.

WRITING

You may be teaching a course in English, or as I have used this example, a course in business letter and report writing. It shows how words can be used for the writer's personal benefit when put together in the right combination.

> Only two cars were entered in an auto race held in Moscow—an American Ford and a Russian Moskvich. The Ford won easily. The next day, however, the Russian newspaper reported, "The Soviet Moskvich placed second while the American Ford was next to last."

I use the following story to illustrate the necessity of "clarity" in writing and to emphasize the importance of not writing over the head of your reader. While this story is funny it also has an important moral.

> The story concerns a plumber who was having problems clearing drains and thought that he had discovered an effective solution. He found that Hydrochloric Acid worked wonders in clogged drains, but he began to wonder if it could also hurt the drains. So, he wrote the U.S. Bureau of Standards and asked them if they could advise him about the use of Hydrochloric Acid in clearing drain pipes.
>
> The Bureau wrote:
>
> "The efficiency of Hydrochloric Acid is indisputable, but the corrosive residue is incompatible with metallic permanence."
>
> A few weeks went by and in came another letter from the plumber thanking the Bureau for okaying the method.
>
> The Bureau, worried, wrote again—this time more emphatically. "We cannot assume responsibility for the production of toxic and noxious residue with Hydrochloric Acid and suggest that you use an alternate method."
>
> A month went by and then came another letter from the plumber: "Yep," he wrote, "the acid was working just fine and he couldn't thank the Bureau enough for recommending it to him."
>
> This time the Bureau did what it should have done when it received his first letter. It wrote:

"Quit using Hydrochloric Acid. It eats the Hell out of the pipes."

HOME ECONOMICS

If you are seeking some humor for a home economics class, you might select this story from the book to brighten your class lectures:

Heard about the new recipe for sponge cake? You *borrow* all the ingredients.

ECONOMICS

An economist is a person who knows more about money than the people who have it.

MUSIC

A music teacher may find that this joke is useful from the classification, "Music."

"I'm warning you," (you tell a difficult pupil) "if you don't behave yourself, I'll tell your parents you have talent."

BIOLOGY

You are explaining a dissection to your class and cite a story about one of your freshman biology students who displayed unusual coolness and who sharpened her technique to the keen edge as the semester progressed.

I noticed (you say) that every incision, every thrust of the blade was swift, clean and unfaltering. Clearly the girl had a natural gift and easily surpassed everyone in the class. When I finally asked her, "Rita, is your father a surgeon?" she replied, "No, sir. But he's the best butcher in (your town)."

CIVICS

There are many categories dealing with government in this

book, including "Government," "America," etc. A good selection to illustrate some phase of class programming could be this one dealing with government:

This is a Democratic Country—the only place where you can say what you think without thinking.

MATHEMATICS

"You know, women have a passion for arithmetic. They divide their ages by two, double the price of their clothes, triple their husband's salaries, and add five years to the ages of their best friends."

One of my pupils remarked that Jeanne gets straight A's in French because her parents are Parisians and they speak French at home.

"Then I ought to get an A in geometry," said another student. "My parents are square and they talk in circles."

SCIENCE

I asked one of my students to tell me what is the greatest change that takes place when water becomes ice.

He said "price."

Science has been taking great strides forward. Now it is only 50 years behind the comic books.

The only trouble with science today is that it is slowly filling our homes with appliances that are smarter than we are.

BOTANY

During an Arbor Day planting program, one of the youngsters remarked about the fertilizer, "Is that the only scent it comes in?"

BUSINESS EDUCATION

Capital is money the other fellow has. *Labor* is getting it away from him.

Business is always good for those who prepare the statistics.

Part Two

HUMOR

BY CLASSIFICATION

A

Absent Minded (See Charity, Memory)

1. The nurse entered the professor's room and said softly, "It's a boy, sir."

The professor looked up from his desk.

"Well," he said, "What does he want?"

2. "I have an excellent memory," boasted the professor, "but there are three things I cannot remember: names, faces, and—I guess I forgot what the third thing is."

3. It's good to look at the brighter side of things, but it can be carried to the ridiculous. There was an absent-minded professor who had one of those perennially cheerful wives. One evening the professor picked up his cigar from the ashtray and put the lighted end in his mouth. He snatched it out and hurled it across the room, screeched, spat, thundered into the kitchen, dove headfirst into the sink and then lay there face up running cold water into his mouth from the tap.

And all the while his wife, with one hand folded gently into the palm of the other, followed him, smiling sweetly and saying:

"How fortunate you were, dear, to discover it so soon!"

Achievement (See Awards, Diploma, Graduation)

4. Two centuries ago, when a great man appeared, people looked for God's purpose in him; today we look for his press agent.

—Daniel J. Boorstin, "The Image."

5. If what you did yesterday still looks big to you, you haven't done much today.

Accounting (See Business Education, Mathematics)

6. "There's no sense in teaching my son to count over 100," the well-to-do father told the teacher. "He can hire accountants to do his bookkeeping."

"That may be true, Mr. Jones, "the teacher replied. "But he may want to play golf someday."

7. The accountants in group session were discussing procedures and practices.

"How many sets of books is it necessary for a business to keep?" asked one.

"As many as there are partners," replied the instructor.

Adolescence (See Children, High School, Teenagers)

8. Adolescence is that period when many children feel that their parents should be told the facts of life.

9. "Girls grow up so quickly," sighed a mother. "One day you look into your closet—and your favorite dress is gone."

10. An adolescent is a youngster who is old enough to dress himself if he could just remember where he dropped his clothes.

11. An adolescent is a youngster who is old enough to get up in the morning but not quite sure how to progress from there.

12. Adolescence: That wonderful age when boys discover girls and girls discover they have been discovered.

Adult Education (See Children, Parenthood, Teenagers)

13. Adult education is what goes on in a household containing teenage children.

14. Among those things which are so simple that even a child can operate them are parents.

15. No one is too old to learn and that may be why so many keep putting it off.

Advice

16. The trouble with good advice is that it usually interferes with our plans.

—E. W. Howe

17. Man doesn't start giving good advice until he's too old to set a bad example.

18. Be careful when you point your finger at anyone for his sins or misdoings, for then you have three fingers pointing back at yourself.

19. Socrates was a Greek philosopher who went around giving good advice. They killed him.

20. I hate to take advice from somebody who needs it himself.

21. Most of us would get along well if we used the advice that we give others.

22. Don't worry if your grades are low
And your rewards are few.
Remember that the mighty oak
Was once a nut like you.

—Keith Peterson (Brookings, S. Dak.)
Boy's Life

23. Thomas Jefferson's advice: "Don't put off until tomorrow what you can do today. If you enjoy it today, you can do it again tomorrow."

24. Advice is seldom welcome. Those who need it most, like it least.

—Samuel Johnson

35

Age-Aging (See Adolescence, Middle-Age, Teenagers, Time, Youth)

25. A professor is getting old when he inspects the food in the cafeteria instead of the waitress.

26. An old timer recalls when "going to pot" meant you were getting a bit seedy.

27. An old timer is one who can remember when the headquarters for the beat generation was the woodshed.

28. An old timer is one who remembers when a college student was satisfied to have just a picture of his girl in his room.

29. Age will ruin a choice steak or an egg, but it has little to do with works of art.

30. Remember, these trying times in school will be "the old days" in just a few years.

31. The next time you get the feeling that you'd like to be young again, think of writing those long term papers yourself.

32. You know you are getting old when you find yourself offering good advice instead of setting bad examples.

33. You're old if you went to college to take courses rather than buildings.

34. By the time an instructor finds greener pastures, he can't climb the fence.

35.   An old timer is one who remembers when a demonstration only meant that someone was trying to sell you a new vacuum cleaner.

36.   By the time the average man learns where he stands, his knees have buckled.

37.   The three ages of man: school tablet, aspirin tablet and stone tablet.

38.   A person your own age always looks older than yourself.

39.   Growing old is only a state of mind .... brought on by gray hairs, false teeth, wrinkles, a big belly, short breath and all over feeling of being constantly bushed.

40.   Some say that even in the Stone Age when a woman wrote down her age, she chiseled a little.

41.   Age brings wisdom and tolerance. You don't mind being called middle-aged when you no longer are.

Agriculture

42.   The teacher was giving a lecture on agriculture and as part of it tried to explain how birds and insects damage crops.

Little Tommy did not appear to be interested, so the teacher pointed to him and said, "Now, Tommy, which are the worst, worms or crows?"

"I don't know," answered Tommy. "I haven't had crows."

43.   A fifth-grader gave this definition of a farmer: "A man outstanding in his field."

44.   Corn is a commodity that's sold by the bushel in the Midwest, by the fifth in the South and by the hour in TV.

—Ray Sackett

45. A farm is what a city man dreams of at 5 P.M.—but never at 5 A.M.

46. "Did you ever meet with an accident?" inquired the student of the farmer.

"No," said the farmer, then added as an afterthought, "a mule kicked in two of my ribs once and a year ago a rattlesnake bit me on the leg."

"Great Scott," gasped the student "don't you consider those accidents?"

"Naw," said the farmer, "They done it on purpose."

47. Teacher: "How much are these tomatoes?"

Farmer: "They are 40 cents a pound."

Teacher: "Did you raise them yourself?"

Farmer: "Yes, sir, I certainly did. They were only 35 cents yesterday."

Alibis (See School, Students)

48. "My books were stolen from my locker two weeks ago, and I haven't been able to do any homework since."

49. "John Smith is sick and can't attend school today. He asked me to telephone you."

"All right. Who's this speaking?"

"This is my brother."

50. Johnnie was late for school one day. The teacher asked the cause of the delay.

Johnnie explained: "my mother's sick."

The teacher, thinking it might be contagious asked, "What does the doctor say it is?"

"A girl."

51. It was a delightful day and four high school girls skipped morning classes to go for a drive. After lunch they reported to a teacher that their car had had a flat tire on the way to school that morning.

Much to their relief, she smiled understandingly and said: "Girls, you missed a test this morning. Please take seats apart from one another and get out your pencils."

When the girls were settled and waiting expectantly, the teacher passed out paper and continued. "No talking. Now write the answer to this question: 'Which tire was flat?' "

52. A teacher received this note from a mother to excuse her child from school.

"Please excuse Carol for being absent. She has a virus infection. I am having her shot tonight."

53. A teacher was constantly receiving incomplete assignments from one of her students who had a high I.Q. So, she called him in to talk with her about it.

"I really want to do all the work," he said "but I get tired before I get there."

54. "What a terrible evening sobbed the instructor's wife after they had returned from a party."

"Why?" asked the husband. "I had a good time, didn't I?"

"A good time!" stormed the wife. "Imagine an instructor placing a burning cigarette in each ear, yelling 'I'm a missile!' at the top of your lungs and then diving into the swimming pool with your clothes on. Why?"

"Because," mumbled the instructor, "the cigarettes were burning my ears."

Alumni (See Graduation, Parent)

55. About three weeks before an annual college-club dinner, an alumnus received a letter from the club president asking him to serve on the reception committee. A scarlet ribbon marked RECEPTION COMMITTEE was enclosed. The alumnus had not intended to go—the dinners were usually a bore. But since he had been asked to be on the committee, he couldn't turn it down.

By the time he arrived, almost 400 members of the club were there, each wearing a scarlet ribbon marked RECEPTION COMMITTEE.

—Henry E. Leabo
Quips and Quotes

56. A class reunion is when people get together to see who's falling apart.

57.   The class reunion I was at
Was really rather gloomy
My schoolmates were so old and fat
Most of them hardly knew me.

58.   Wife to husband: Obviously you laid it on pretty thick at your class reunion last week. Here's a letter from your Alma Mater suggesting that you endow the school.

59.   "Professor," said the old grad at the class reunion, "I want to do something for the college. In what studies did I excel?"
"In my class," replied the professor, "you slept most of the time."
"A good suggestion," said the grad unabashed. "I'll build a dormitory."

60.   Two grads met at the 20th reunion. One had been on top of the class, the other had a tough time getting his diploma, having had particular trouble with math. The latter seemed to have prospered.
"Joe," said the top man, "you seem to have done exceptionally well. How did you do it?"
"Well," said Joe, "after graduation, I realized I was pretty dumb, and I had better get into some line where I didn't need to be smart like you and some of the others. So I found a product I could make for one dollar and sell to the public for $5.00 and believe me that steady 400% really mounts up over the years.

Ambition (See Achievement, Determination)

61.   "He drove straight to his goal," cried the political orator. "He looked neither to the right nor to the left, but pressed forward, moved by a definite purpose. Neither friend nor foe could delay him or turn him from his course. All who crossed his path did so at their own peril! What would you call such a man?"
"A truck driver," shouted someone from the audience.

—Illustrated Weekly of India

62.   The seven stages of ambition:
To be like Dad; to be an engineer; to pilot an airplane; to be famous; to become a millionaire; to make both ends meet; to hang on long enough to draw a pension.

—Farm Journal

63. Having too much ambition can cause headaches. Many a man has taken too much aspirin because of too much aspiration.

64. They say that to get ahead you have to know somebody, and that's true. You have to know yourself.

65. You can never get ahead of anyone you're trying to get even with.

66. Parents always have been able to tell what occupations their children find appealing, ever since that first little boy declared that he wanted to become a fireman. But hear how this ten-year-old girl has her future programmed: "Mom, you know what I want to be? First, a lifeguard. Then a model. Then a dancer. Then a singer. Then an actress. Then, I guess, an old hag."

67. If you expect ever to have any pull, you'll have to push for it.

68. I've been hunting that silver lining for more than half a century. Why is it always easier to find in someone else's cloud?

69. Getting up in the morning is largely a matter of mind over mattress.

70. Perhaps the most difficult instrument any go-getter has to play is second fiddle.

71. Ambition that goes to seed is defined as "contentment."

Americans, America (See Citizenship)

72. The difference between America's capitalistic system and the others is that the rest of the systems promise all the good things we've already got.

73. American people don't actually want a cheaper car. They want an expensive car that costs less.

74. Let's join the chorus of those who are singing about the problems of the United States.

Let's admit it. We've got problems no other nation has. For example:

No other nation in the world has any problems caused by a surplus of food.

No other nation has such traffic congestion because so many people own their own automobiles.

· In no other country do people take so many holidays and have so much leisure time in which to spend the money which they earn; more money than wage earners get in any other country.

And no other country has as one of its chief medical problems the fact that so many people are overweight because of the abundance they enjoy.

—Parts Pups

75. In America we compliment a woman by telling her she looks like a million dollars. But think what would happen to you in Britain if you told an Englishwoman she looked like a million pounds.

76. This is the country of faith. On the installment plan you can buy what you can't afford. On the stock market you can sell what you don't own. And on the income tax return they take away what you haven't borrowed yet.

77. He wants to run his own business.
He wants to select his own doctor.
He wants to make his own bargains.
He wants to buy his own insurance.
He wants to select his own reading matter.
He wants to provide for his own old age.
He wants to make his own contracts.
He wants to select his own charities.
He wants to educate his children as he wishes.
He wants to make his own investments.
He wants to select his own friends.

He wants to provide his own recreation.
He wants to compete freely in the market place.
He wants to grow by his own efforts.
He wants to profit from his own errors.
He wants to take part in the competition of ideas.
He wants to be a man of goodwill.
What kind of a man is he?
He's an American, that's what kind!
—*Maryville, Calif. Appeal-Democrat*

78.   America is a system under which a man pays a quarter to park his car so he won't be fined a dollar while spending a dime for a nickel cup of coffee.

79.   America is the only country in the world where you can go on the air and kid politicians and where politicians go on the air and kid the people.   —*Smiles*

80.   This country originally cited the Pursuit of Happiness as a goal. It wasn't until years later that the politicians offered to catch it for the people.

—*The Scrap Book,* 1959

Animals

81.   The wife asked her professor husband to take the stray cat off somewhere and lose it. So he put the cat in a basket and drove off into the country.

"Did you lose the cat?" asked the wife when he returned.

"Lose the cat!" said the professor. "If I hadn't followed her, I'd never have made it back home!"

82.   A kindergarten teacher was asked by one of her small charges whether the rabbit they were playing with was a boy or a girl. Not wanting to be drawn into a birds-and-bees discussion, she said she didn't know.

Another youngster volunteered, "I know how we can find out."

Bracing herself for the worst, the teacher almost reached to put her hand over his mouth. But he blurted out: "We can take a vote!"

Animals

83.   I recently read about a Central Park Zoo hippo having a baby. I understand the hardest part was getting her into the cab for the trip to the hospital.

84.   The first graders on a field trip saw a flock of birds about to migrate. The teacher explained that they were noisy and excited because they were starting out on a long journey: "What do you suppose they are saying?" she asked.

A shy little girl spoke up: "I 'magine the mother birds are telling their children they'd better go to the bathroom first."

85.   Teacher: "... and from the skunk we get fur, isn't that right, Johnny?"

Johnny: "I'll say so! As fur as possible."

86.   A kangaroo is nature's initial effort to produce a cheer-leader.

87.   "Oh, what a lovely cow," said the young student from the city during a field trip to a farm. "But why hasn't it got any horns?"

"There are many reasons," replied the farmer. "Some cows don't have them until later in life. Others have them removed. While still other breeds are born without them. This one doesn't have horns mainly because it's a horse."

88.   "Edward, name six animals that inhabit the Arctic region."

"Three seals and three polar bears."

89.   Teacher: "Why did Noah take two of each kind of animal into the ark?"

Student: "I guess he didn't believe the story about the stork."

90.   Teacher: "It says here that more than 5,000 camels are used each year to make paint brushes."

Second Teacher: "Isn't is amazing what they can teach animals to do these days."

91. On a trip to the zoo, a youngster stared at the kangaroo in stunned silence. The sign read: "Native of Australia."

"Great Heavens!" she exclaimed to her classmate. "My sister married one of them."

92. A student was learning about the different animals that provide people with food.

"If cows give us milk, chickens give us eggs and pigs give us bacon, what do horses give us?"

"Horseradish!" replied one of the students.

93. A kindergarten teacher was showing her children illustrations of a lion and lioness.

"Can anyone tell me the difference between these?" asked the teacher.

"I know," said one little boy. "One just got a haircut."

Appreciation (See Awards, Heroism)

94. The only persons you should want to get even with are those who have helped you.

95. Among the smaller duties of life I hardly know any one more important than that of not praising where praise is not due.

—Sydney Smith

96. "Are you the young man who risked his life to save my son from drowning when he fell through the ice?"

"Yes, ma'am."

"Well, what in the - - - - did you do with his mittens?"

Art-Antiques

97. In the window of a campus antique dealer: "We have a complete line of what you don't need."

98. One way to buy antiques is to buy high-priced furniture on the installment plan and keep it until you have paid for it.

99. Sign in a Junk Yard: We buy junk and sell antiques.

100. The only difference between some antiques and junk is the price.

101. The student artist was showing his pictures to a friend. "Now here's a picture; one of my best, too. When I started out I had no idea what it was going to be."

His roommate looked puzzled. "Tell me, after you got through, how did you find out what it was?"

102. A cynic was standing in front of an exhibition of student art labeled, "Art Objects."

"Well," he announced to the attendant in charge. "I can't say that I blame him."

—Smiles

103. Much modern art looks as if it were done while the artist was having an unpleasant conversation on the telephone.

104. "You were swindled over this Rembrandt," stated the art expert. "This picture is about 50 years old."

"Who cares how old it is," replied the proud owner, "as long as it is a genuine Rembrandt."

105. Sir Winston Churchill, who was known as one of the most famous amateur painters, showed a group of his canvases to a friend.

"Tell me," said the latter, "why is it that you paint only landscapes?"

"Because," replied Churchill, "a tree doesn't complain that I haven't done it justice."

Automation (See Business Education)

106. A student walked up to a vending machine in the student lounge, put in a coin, pressed the button labeled "Coffee, double cream, sugar." No cup appeared, but the nozzles went into action, sending forth coffee, cream and sugar. After the proper amounts had gone down the drain the machine turned off.

"Now that's real automation," exclaimed the student. "This thing even drinks it for you."

107. A teacher told one of his students that he need not ever worry about being replaced by automation. "They haven't invented a machine yet that does absolutely nothing," he said.

108. Automation is man's effort to make work so easy that women can do it all.

109. Automation: A $75-a-week clerk replaced by a $250,000 machine.

110. Automation didn't eliminate red tape—it just perforated it.
—Blantz Brown
Wall Street Journal

Automobiles (See Driving)

111. A student was almost hit by a car which broke away from the curb and, driverless, rolled almost into him.

An instructor came chasing after it and explained that she had been mailing a letter. The student asked why she hadn't put on the emergency.

"What's an emergency about mailing a letter?" she inquired.

112. The outraged music teacher was complaining about having received a bill for $50 from his garage for tuning up his car's engine.

"For heaven's sake!" the teacher bellowed. "Who does the tuning up in this joint—Leonard Bernstein?"

113. A high school student we know was such a poor driver that the traffic department gave him a season ticket.

114. The outlook for automobile trade is excellent. There are still thousands of teacher's homes that haven't been mortgaged to buy cars.

Aviation

115. The traffic was heavy and the smart alec high school student was honking his horn like it was going out of style.

The man in the car alongside looked him over, stuck his head out of the window and asked, "And what else did you get for Christmas?"

116. There was the mad genius who crossed a pedestrian with an automobile and got a lawsuit.

—D.O. Flynn

117. In a downpour, a student saw a little lady kneeling beside her car, halfway through the job of changing a tire. A great rush of sympathy went through him and he parked his car nearby, and went back to finish changing the tire for her. He put on the spare, getting soaking wet. Then, as he began jerking at the jack to let the car down, the little lady whispered: "Oh, gently, please! The athletic coach is taking a nap in the back seat and I wouldn't want to wake him!"

118. New cars these days have a longer guarantee than the students who drive them.

119. The used car dealer was demonstrating an old heap. As he started up a hill he said to the principal, "This is the opportunity of a lifetime."

"Sure is," said the principal. "I can even hear it knocking."

120. One of our colleagues had his new car called back—to correct a defect in his bank account.

121. A lot of traffic problems could be solved with as much horsesense in the car as horsepower under the hood.

122. Strange, but you can't drive a new car down the street without meeting everybody you owe.

Aviation

123. Two high school students were talking of the future. "I'm going to be an air hostess," said one.

"Might be a good idea," said the other student "but wouldn't you meet as many men doing something else?"

"Could be, but not strapped down."

124.   One nice thing about Minnesota winters: Nobody is hijacking planes to fly there.

125.   On a New York-to-Los Angeles flight a teacher's young son nearly drove everyone crazy. He was running up and down the aisle when the stewardess started serving coffee and ran into her, knocking the coffee to the floor.

As she was cleaning up the mess she glanced up at the boy and said, "Look, why don't you run outside and play?"

Awards (See Appreciation)

126.   The teacher won the jackpot on the big quiz show and was so shocked it killed her. The sponsors, good sports that they were, kept their word and shipped her body to Bermuda for two weeks.

127.   The university coed who won the title of the girl with the best belly button will one day be hard put to explain to her grandchildren when they discover the trophy in the bottom of grandma's trunk.

–Claude Eames
Elkhorn Independent

B

Baseball (See Sports)

128.   A student and his very slow girlfriend finally arrived at the baseball game. It was the 7th inning and the score was 0 to 0.

"See?" said the girl. "We didn't miss a thing!"

129.   The teacher had asked her pupils who the nine greatest

Americans were. All pupils had turned in their papers except Johnny.

"Can't you finish your list, Johnny?" asked the teacher.

"I'm still undecided," replied Johnny, "about the first baseman."

130.   College Baseball Pitcher: "I would have pitched a no-hitter except for them 8 homers they got off me."

131.   A no-hit pitcher is a ballplayer who can throw a ball faster than you can shake a stick at.

132.   Several of the umpire's calls had gone against State University, and the coach had discussed each one with the umpire. In the sixth inning, as the umpire told it, a foul ball was hit into the stands. He looked over and saw a woman being carried out on a stretcher.

"Did that ball hit her?" he asked the coach.

In a loud voice the coach yelled. "No! You called it right and she fainted."

133.   The high school coach shouted to his all-star player: "Come on, Mike—hurry up! You're slower than my grandmother, and she's a hundred and four."

Mike: "Who does *she* pitch for?"

134.   When the college baseball manager told his pitcher he was about to be taken out of the game, the pitcher objected, pointing out that he had struck out the next batter his last time to bat.

"Yeh," came the reply, "but that was in the same inning."

135.   A local high school coach who had an ulcer was in the physician's office for a check-up.

"Remember," the doctor said, "don't get excited, don't get mad, and forget about baseball when you're off the field." Then he added.

"By the way, how come you let the pitcher bat yesterday with the tieing run on second and two out in the ninth?"

136.   If the White Sox want more runs they should change their name to Nylons.

Basketball (See Baseball, Sports)

137. College basketball coach to players: "Now remember that basketball develops individuality, initiative, and leadership. Now get out on the floor and do exactly as I told you."

138. Girl: "What position do you play on the school basketball team this season?"
Bench Warmer: "Oh, sort of crouched and bent over."

139. A college senior and his date were watching a basketball game. He pointed to the court and said: "See No. 33 down there. He's going to be our best man next year."
"Oh, darling," she said. "This is so sudden!"

140. There's an easy way to have a successful basketball player in your family—rear one that's seven feet tall.

141. A sports fan reports that since the language on television seems to be getting franker and franker, it won't be long before we'll be hearing what the coach says when his team loses the championship by one point.

Behavior (See Discipline, Manners)

142. "I don't know what I'm going to do about that son of mine," said a parent to the teacher. "He's not really a bad kid, but everything he does gets on my nerves."
"Have you ever thought of buying him a bicycle?"
"No. But do you really think that would improve his behavior?"
"Probably not," replied the teacher. "But it would help to spread it over a wider area."

143. "Well, Glenn," said the little boy's mother as he walked into the kitchen, "were you a good boy at school today?"
"Sure," answered the lad. "How much trouble can you get into standing in a corner all day?"

Biology (See Animals, Nature Study, Science)

144.   Father says his son is at the awkward age. He doesn't know whether to give a girl his seat on the school bus or race her for it.

145.   Teacher discussing behavior of student with principal: "He's from a trouble-free home, is accepted by his group, has a good I.Q., and no emotional disturbances. He's just a stinker."

146.   The problem with many youngsters is being told that it's more important to be dry under the arms than behind the ears.

Biology (See Animals, Nature Study, Science)

147.   Anatomy is something everyone has but it looks better on a girl.

148.   When my friend Rita attempted her first laboratory dissection as a New York University freshman biology student, she displayed unusual coolness. As the semester progressed, she sharpened her technique to a keen edge. Every incision, every thrust of the blade was swift, clean and unfaltering. Clearly, the girl had a natural gift and easily surpassed the performance of everyone else in the class. Her instructor's curiosity was piqued from the beginning, and finally he asked, "Rita, is your father a surgeon?"

"No, sir," she replied, "but he's the best butcher in Brooklyn."
                                        —Mrs. M.N. Grant—*Reader's Digest*

149.   One of my first graders bounced excitedly into class one day and asked, "May I bring a racoon to school tomorrow?"

"A racoon?" I asked surprised. Knowing that many fathers in our area hunted racoons, I continued, "Would it be dead or alive?"

"I don't really know," she said "but I do know if you keep it long enough it will turn into a butterfly."

150.   While instructing her students on the various parts of the body she asked a student if he knew another name for the tiniest veins in our bodies.

"Oh, yes," he replied. "Caterpillars."

151.   When the teacher explained that the human body had about 200 bones, one of the students protested that he had more.

"How many do you have?" Johnnie.

"Probably 50 or 60 more," he said. "We had fish for dinner last night."

Books (See Journalism, Words, Writing)

152.   A rare book is one that comes back after you've loaned it out.

153.   Another good thing about books is that they inspire others to authorship. Did you ever see a child resist the urge to pen his own sentiments on the covers or flysheet of a good book?

154.   Standing in the checkout line of the Vassar cooperative bookshop at the beginning of the term, I was surprised to find that the books for one of my courses cost more than twice as much as those for any other subject. The course? Sociology 257a—Poverty!

—Susan Gooden, *Readers Digest*

155.   In a library, the books that aren't dirty are the ones that are dusty.

—Wildred Beaver

156.   Arnold Glasow: "Some of today's literary drivel is enough to make you burn your library card."

—*Chicago Tribune*

157.   Did you hear about the new book club for people who hate to read? If you join, they promise not to send you a book every month.

158.   A librarian in an elementary school is guided by a principle that motivates all children's librarians: Find the right book for the right child at the right time.

She was overjoyed, of course, when little Billy a first grader, chose a book and explained that he wanted that particular book that particular day.

"Oh, good, Billy!" she exclaimed as she signed his card for the book. He was proud that he had pleased.

"Yes, it's just the right size to fit into my lunch bucket," he explained.

159.   Used Books for Sale. Excellent condition. By old lady who read only 50 words a minute.

160.   Men do not understand books until they have had a certain amount of life.

—Ezra Pound

161.   Remember when comic books used to be called "family albums."

162.   When better books are suppressed more people will read them.

Board of Education (See College, School)

163.   The trouble with most boards of education is that they are not used in the right place.

—*Chicago Tribune*

Botany (See Biology, Science)

164.   The following is the daily record of a fifth grader's bean plant science experiment.

3/16 . . . Two of them had grown one-inch roots, one of them had half-inch roots. They have been planted two days ago.

3/17 . . . Four of the beans have come out of the top of the ground.

3/18 . : . Now all of my beans have come out of the ground.

3/23 . . . Leaves are starting to appear on the bean.

3/27 . . . Now I have leaves on one bean.

3/30 . . . They are starting to wilt

4/1 . . . They're dead.

—Louise Crytzer, Lundhurst, Ohio

165.   The children were taking part in an Arbor Day planting program and were using generous amounts of fertilizer. One youngster asked, "Is that the only scent that it comes in?"

Business Education (See Computer)

166. A student was asked to define "capitalism." His reply was: "I am not sure I can give you a good definition of capitalism, as I am not too clear on what it is, but I understand there is a lot of it going on in this country and if we don't do something about it, we are going to get in real trouble."

—Carl Carlson

167. Capital is money the other fellow has. Labor is getting it away from him.

168. Business is always good for those who prepare the statistics.

169. You can be a success in business even with a low I.Q., if you have a high "I will."

170. In discussing business, the professor told the story of the Sultan who had 20 beautiful wives. He would sit in his chamber and when he had picked out a wife he wanted, he would send a 10-year-old boy, called a "runner" after her.

As time went on, the Sultan lived to be 121 years old, while the "runner" died at the age of 40.

The moral of this story is that business never hurt anyone. It's the running after it that wears men out."

171. "There are always three kinds of people in business," said the college professor. "Those who make things happen. Those who watch things happen. And those who don't know what's happening."

172. Overheard outside the door of a typing class: "Gay is such a slow typist, every time the little bell rings on her typewriter, she thinks its time that the class be dismissed."

173. "When I walk through the typists' class," remarked the principal,"I feel like a piece of uranium approaching a whole battery of Geiger counters."

"What do you mean?" asked the typing teacher.

"Well, the closer I get, the faster the clicks."

174. Two women students were discussing a recently-purchased office machine.

"I know it does the work of three men," one said. "But I'd rather have the men."

175. Teacher to inefficient student: "Are you really going to quit this class, Miss Clark, or are you just saying that to brighten my day."

176. "Business is never so healthy as when, like a chicken, it must do a certain amount of scratching for what it gets."

—Henry Ford

177. Sign in a business establishment: "We're a non-profit organization. We don't mean to be—but we are."

C

Character

178. An inexhaustible good nature is one of the most precious gifts of heaven, spreading itself like oil over the troubled sea of thought, and keeping the mind smooth and equable in the roughest weather.

—Washington Irving

179. "Character is the total of thousands of small daily strivings to live up to the best that is in us," wrote A. G. Trudeau. "Character is the final decision to reject whatever is demeaning to oneself or to others and with confidence and honesty to choose the right."

180. We are more than half what we are by imitation. The great point is to choose good models and to study them with care.

—Lord Chesterfield

181. An unbiased person: someone who has the same bias as we have.

—The Tulsa (Texas) *Herald*

182. If you are satisfied just to get by, step aside for the man who isn't.

183. How a man plays the game shows something of his character. How he loses shows all of it.

184. A man reveals his character more surely when he tells jokes in private than when he prays in public.

185. Admitting that you are all wrong when you are all wrong, makes you an all-right guy.

186. Imagination was given to man to compensate him for what he is not; and a sense of humor was provided to console him for what he is.

187. When you try to make an impression, that's the impression you make.

188. Character is not made in a crisis—it is only exhibited then.

189. Character is made by what you stand for; reputation by what you fall for.

190. A man is known by the company he thinks nobody knows he's keeping.

Chemistry (See Science)

191. There are fast-talking slow thinkers and slow-talking fast thinkers, and you have to watch out for both of them.

Chemistry (See Science)

192. A teacher asked his class what they could tell him about "nitrates."

One student raised his hand and said: "Well ... er ... they are a lot cheaper than day rates."

193. A professor asked his chemistry class what they thought would be the world's most important chemical discovery.

One student replied that he thought it would be a universal solvent ... something that would dissolve anything and everything.

"That's a good suggestion," replied the, professor. "But tell me, what do you plan to keep it in."

194. "Can you tell me, Mr. Smith one of the outstanding contributions that chemistry has given to the world?"

"Yessir. Blondes."

195. They say that man is worth more today than ever before. He should be. The cost of the chemicals in his body has gone up.

Children (See also Adolescence, Education, Kindergarten, School, Teaching)

196. Many a house has been "bugged" by miniature snooping devices for several years. They repeat every word in school.

197. Johnny started school and within two weeks the teacher sent home a note containing the following: "Young Johnny is more than I can handle. I am forced to ask your help."

The next day the mother sent her answer: "Listen, all those years I had him alone, did I ask *your* help?"

198. Teacher: "Jerry, why is your composition on milk only a half-page long when I asked for two pages?"

Jerry: "I wrote on 'condensed milk.'"

199. The only things that children wear out faster than shoes are parents and teachers.

200. I know I don't get the best marks in school, Dad, but do you get the best salary at your office?"

201. The behavior of some children suggests that their parents embarked on the sea of matrimony without a paddle.

—Mason City (Ia.) Globe-Gazette

202. A child is growing up when he stops asking where he came from and starts refusing where he is going.

203. A teacher was questioning some boys. "Can you take your warm overcoats off?" he asked.

"Yes sir," they replied.

"Can the bear take his warm overcoat off?"

"No sir."

"Why not?"

There was a long silence. Finally one boy spoke up. "Please, sir, because only God knows where the buttons are."

204. A little boy ran into the house, jumped across the bed, turned over the television, and jumped on the kitchen table.

"Mama, Mama!" he shouted. "I made an A in school."

"In what?" asked his mother.

"Self-control," said the son.

205. Junior brought home a note from school. They want a written excuse for his presence.

Children (See also Adolescence, Education, Kindergarten, School, Teaching)

206. Willie to teacher. "I don't understand my mother. When I'm noisy, she spanks me, but when I'm quiet, she takes my temperature."

—Mrs. Floyd Begley, Kentucky

207. A first grader came home from school one day with a zero marked on his paper. His mother exclaimed, "Jimmy why did you get that zero?"

Jimmy responded, "That's no zero, Mommy. The teacher ran out of stars and she gave me the moon."

208. Today's bright child may well ask which came first: "the chicken or Colonel Sanders?"

209. A father took his little boy to the zoo where they were watching the elephants.

"Pop," asked the child "where do elephants come from? And don't give me that stork routine."

210. A teacher once asked a youngster what happened when there was an eclipse of the moon.

"A lot of people," answered the boy "come out and look at it."

211. One of the first things a kid learns in school is that the other kids get an allowance.

212. The child of wealthy parents was asked in school to write a story about a poor family. She began:

"This family was very poor. The mommy and daddy were poor. The maid and butler and cook were poor. . . ."

213. "Mike," said the teacher "what is your greatest ambition?"
"To wash my mother's ears!" promptly replied Mike.

214. Overheard In the Teachers' Lounge: "Not only is he the worst-behaved child in my class—he also has a perfect attendance record!"

—L.J. Goodyear

Children (See also Adolescence, Education, Kindergarten, School, Teaching)

215. A small girl, says Emily M. Smith, was entertaining visitors who arrived while her mother was still upstairs.

After appraising the child one woman turned to the other and said, "Not very p-r-e-t-t-y."

"No," interjected the child, "but awfully s-m-a-r-t."

216. Overheard in a school cafeteria: One boy said to the other: "Okay, let's run away from home—should we ask your mother or mine to drive us?"

—Grit

217. Two little boys were wandering over the countryside near the Sunnyglade Nudist Camp. They came to a fence posted with the sign: "No trespassing—Nudist Camp." And as they climbed over the fence, one commented, "My big brother says when I learn to read there won't be no more surprises."

218. A boy is like a mosquito. The minute he stops making noise, you know he must be getting into something.

—Earl Wilson

219. A housewife was watching the launching of a spaceship on television. She watched the intense activity of the ground control team, the hurrying of people this way and that, the seconds of countdown being ticked off, the suspense of the last few instants. Then there was an eruption of smoke and flame; the rocket rose slowly and accelerated away until it was lost in the distance.

"Hm," she muttered to herself. "It's just like getting Billy off to school."

220. "Kids are getting much more involved in world problems these days. There's a 10-year-old in my neighborhood who already has an ulcerette."

221. If you don't think your children can count, try giving them different allowances.

—The Altamont (Ill) *News*

222. Childhood is that wonderful time when all you need to do to lose weight is bathe.

223. In the United States, parent and teacher look at their tots and think: "Maybe he'll grow up and be President."
In Europe they just think: "Maybe he'll grow up."

224. Children have become so expensive that only the poor can afford them.

225. When asked why he got so dirty a little boy told his teacher:
"Gee, I'm a lot closer to the ground than you are."

226. Teacher: "I am afraid your little brother is awfully shy. He hasn't moved from that one spot all afternoon."
Big Sister: "Oh, he isn't shy. This is the first time he ever wore a necktie, and he thinks he is tied to something."

227. Toys are what children amuse themselves with when there is nothing left to wreck.
—The Lapeer County (Mich) *Press*

228. In my day, claims the supervisor, a wayward child was straightened out by being bent over.

229. Everything in the home these days is controlled by a switch except the children.
—The Budget, Sugar Creek, Ohio

230. Every bright boy asks for more than he expects to get.
—William Feather

231. Teacher: "That child!"
Second Teacher: "What now?"
Teacher: "She wanted to know where baby storks come from."

Children (See also Adolescence, Education, Kindergarten, School, Teaching)

232. "So God has sent you two more little brothers, Sally," said her teacher to the small girl.

"Yes," she replied, "and He knows where the money is coming from, too. I heard Daddy say so."

233. Learning her safety lesson a six-year-old said: "Even if you cross the street on a green light, you should be on the allergic!"

234. These days, a child who knows the value of a dollar must be mighty discouraged.

235. Psychiatrist: "Tell me Madam, is your son a behavior problem?"

Mother: "I don't know. He has never behaved."

236. Mealtime is that period when kids sit down to continue eating.

237. "This looks too complicated for a young child," the teacher said to the salesman in the toy department.

"It's an educational toy designed to adjust a child to live in the world today," explained the clerk. "Any way he puts it together . . . it's wrong."

238. "Thanks very much," said the teacher to her pupil. "I must call this afternoon and thank your mother for those eight beautiful apples."

"Please," said Tommy "do you mind thanking her for twelve."

239. Definition of a child: "A short human being who stands between you and the television set."

240. At a certain age everything a boy touches turns to property damage.

–Chan Harris in the
Door County Advocate.

241. Kids are like canoes. They both go straight when paddled from the rear.

Citizenship (See America, Americans)

242. A youngster working on a lesson was trying to figure out what a "full life" would include. After the teacher had given him some "hints," his face lit up and he wrote: "Recess."

Citizenship (See America, Americans)

243. Preparing for a citizenship test, a European teacher was shown a photo of Abraham Lincoln by her son and asked to identify it.
"That's Abe Lincoln," she said confidently.
Then he showed her a picture of bewigged George Washington.
She looked at the picture perplexedly and then answered, "That's his wife."

244. After years of study and the untangling of much red tape, the teacher refugee couple finally managed to gain their citizenship.
The husband rushed into the kitchen with the good news.
"Anna, Anna," he shouted. "At last we are American citizens."
"How wonderful, how wonderful," Anna replied. "Now you can do the dishes."

245. A citizen is a man who demands better roads, bigger schools, a new post office, and lower taxes.

246. "Are you a natural born citizen of the United States?"
"Naw, Caesarean."

City Life

247. Teacher: "Can someone tell me why it is believed that the people in big cities are not as smart as those in smaller towns?"
Student: "That's where the population is the most dense."

248. The reason American cities are prosperous is that there is no place to sit down.

—A.J. Talley

249. Can you remember when it was cheaper to park a car in a city than drive it?

—*The Huntingburg* (Ind.) *Independence*

250.   Every city is filled with dreamers who long for a farm . . . until they get it.

251.   "I have just read that a man is run over in New York City every half hour," remarked a teacher to his class in Civics.

"Poor fellow," remarked one of the students.

Civilization (See America—Americans)

252.   Civilization has brought us this far: Now when a man's wife nags him, he goes to a club instead of reaching for one.

253.   Mohandas Gandi was once asked: "What do you think of Western Civilization?" "I think it would be a good idea," he replied.

254.   The true test of civilization is, not the census, nor the size of cities, nor the crops, but the kind of man that the country turns out.

—Emerson

255.   All who have meditated on the art of governing mankind have been convinced that the fate of empires depends on the education of youth.

—Aristotle

256.   It's fine for colleges to offer courses on "What Contemporary Civilization Is," but we would like to know where it is, too.

257.   Today's big civilization challenge is for the masses to adopt the ideas of the minorities.

College (See Alumni, Education, Schools, Students, Student Demonstration, Study, Teachers)

258.   College Years is the only vacation a boy gets between his mother and his wife.

259.   College education is more than a mastery of tricks which bring early success; more than a secret magic, knowledge of which will immediately transform one's personality and confer fame and fortune. Shoddiness is the result when shortcuts are sought in matters of mental growth. The only time wasted in education is that spent trying to save time. There should be no haste, crowding or cramming. Mastery of any subject requires years of familiarity with it. The formal training one receives at college is but the introduction.

—Joseph L. Lennon in *Columbia*

260. Ad in the classified column of a college newspaper: "Will the person who stole the jar of alcohol from Room 303 kindly return the appendix. No questions asked."

261. College education won't hurt any man—providing he's willing to learn something afterwards.

262. Sending a youngster through college these days is very educational. It teaches his parents how to do without a lot of things.

263. Son in college applying pressure for more money from home: "I cannot understand why you call yourself a kind father, when you haven't sent me a check for three weeks. What kind of kindness do you call that?"

"That," replied the father "is unremitting kindness."

264. A rich old lady was paying her nephew's college bills, and her friend asked her if it were expensive.

"Well," she said "the languages run a bit high. This check covered $10 for English, $20 for Latin and $105 for Scotch."

—*Lumber Dealer's News*

265. An old college grad is one who thinks college is for education, not agitation.

266. Most college campuses are so crowded, if a student wants to be alone, he has to go to class.

267.   "Does your boy go to college . . . or can you sleep easy at night."

—Alvie Phillips in the
Burlington Standard Press

268.   There might be fewer sitdowns on college campuses if the sitdowners had to sit out a semester.

269.   Modern universities face two serious problems: too many dropouts and not enough kickouts.

270.   One girl to another: "I wrote to 65 colleges for admission and this one has the best rating—1,762 boys and 250 girls."

271.   People used to go to college to get polish—now they go to drink it.

272.   Elbert Hubbard: "You can lead a boy to college but you cannot make him think."

—*Chicago Tribune*

273.   Two college students were talking about a mutual friend. One of them said: "He just don't plan for the future at all. He's getting married next month and hasn't even found her a job."

274.   Bill: "I wish you fellows wouldn't call me Big Bill."
Phil: "Why not?"
Bill: "These college names stick—and I'm going to be a doctor."

—Leon Smith
Hague, Virginia

275.   College applicants are being asked if they plan to concentrate on tests or protests.

276.   There was a time when college kids thought they were living dangerously when they cut classes.

277. The *Catholic Digest* reports that "sending your boy to college is like sending your clothes to the laundry—you get out what you put in, but may not recognize it."

278. A University of Wisconsin—Oshkosh student writes that a classmate, who was more often asleep than awake in class, was nudged by the professor.

"I don't mind you going to sleep," the prof said, "but it hurts when you don't say 'good-night'."

—Ed Liska in the
Chilton Times—Journal

279. The businessman met a friend on the street corner and they started talking. "Say," commented the friend. "I understand your son is in college now. How is he making it?"

"He's not," was the reply.

"Oh?" was the comment.

"Nope, I'm making it and he's spending it."

280. An intellectual university student decided to write a thesis on a provocative subject: "Psycho-Analytical Synthesis of the Application of Ecological Transcendentalism to the Motivation and Behavior Patterns of Adolescent Females."

In brief, "How girls grow up."

281. A college student's father said that he got a letter from his son at college whose handwriting was so bad that all he could recognize was the dollar signs.

282. It takes a college student 20 minutes longer to say what he thinks than what he knows.

283. Asked why it was no problem to get money from his father while other students found it difficult, a college freshman replied: "It's a snap. I just threaten to come home."

—*Reader's Digest* contributed by
Walter J. Bartozek

284.   Pam: "What is your brother going to be when he gets out of college?"

June: "Very old."

285.   It's a shame colleges don't teach everything that some of the graduates think they know.

286.   Colleges should try working their way through some of the students.

287.   "I want my son out of this no-good college," a father shouted at the college president.

"But he is at the head of his class," remarked the president.

"That's why I think this is a no-good college!"

288.   A professor who habitually misplaced his glasses entered a restaurant one day without them. He called over the busboy and asked him to read the menu for him.

The boy tried hard and then said: "Sorry, sir, I can't read the menu either. I guess I'm as dumb as you are."

289.   Will Rogers' wit was already well developed when the humorist was a college freshman. During one of his first classes, the professor asked him, "Where are your books?"

"I ain't got none," replied Will.

"What would you think of a man going to work without any tools?" asked the professor.

"I'd say he was the boss," quipped Will.

Conscience (See Traits)

290.   The teacher asked his unruly student: "Don't you ever listen to the voice of conscience?"

"I don't think so," was the reply. "What channel is it on?"

—Donny Ryland, Quips and Quotes

291.   Conscience: The still small voice that makes us feel still smaller.

Conservation (See Ecology)

292. An instructor was lecturing on ecology. "Don't suppose there's a person in the house who has done a single thing to conserve our timber resources?" he inquired.

A meek voice from the rear of the hall timidly retorted: "I once shot a woodpecker."

Consultant

293. Screams piercing the air attested to the fact that Harry's tomcat was indeed the cat's meow. But after numerous complaints from the neighbors, Harry allowed a vet to render the cat fit to guard a sultan's harem.

"I'll bet," ventured one of Harry's neighbors weeks later, "that the ex-tom of yours just lies on the hearth now and gets fat."

"No," said Harry, "he still goes out. But now he is a consultant."

Conventions

294. The hotel clerk said to the convention delegates: "We have only one room with a bath, but it's taken. Would you mind sharing a bath with another man?"

"Why, of course not," said the delegate. "Not as long as he stays at his end of the tub."

295. The keynoter at a big school convention began, "Welcome all of you sleepy-eyed registrants. Let's wake up and start the bull rolling."

296. The road to hell is paved with good conventions!

Cost of Living (See Income)

297. It takes more than a sheepskin these days to keep the wolf from the door.

298. Airline schedules, tuition and babies are all alike. They're subject to change without notice.

299. Teacher struggling with the bills to his wife: "We should have saved during the depression so we could live through this prosperity."

300. Fellow colleague: "No wonder I can never get ahead. I'm constantly keeping myself in the pink and my finances out of the red."

301. The teacher's wife told her husband leaving for a shopping trip: "Forget about the large economy size. Get the small expensive package we can afford."

302. Two can live as cheaply as one. My wife and I can live as cheaply as our daughter in college.

303. Most teachers don't worry about the wolf any more. They just feed him on installments.

304. Despite the complaints about the high cost of living, most people still think it's worth it.

—Changing Times

305. Textbook Note: Living on a budget is the same as living beyond your means, except that you keep records.

306. Samuel Butler once said: "All progress is based on the universal innate desire on the part of every organism to live beyond his income."

307. What this country needs is a sanforized dollar.

—California Builder and *Engineer*

308. Sign in a fraternity: "Eat, drink and be merry, for tomorrow it will probably cost more."

309. Most of us would be glad to pay as we go, if we could only catch up from paying as we've gone.

—Kiwanis Magazine

310. The cost of living has risen so much that some of the merchants in our college town are thinking of moving their bargain basement up to the third floor.

Courage (See Traits, Valor)

311. Let's face it. Our real problem is not the high cost of living—it's the cost of high living.

— *The Athens* (Ala.) *Limeston Democracy*

312. "It's no trick to meet expenses," Professor Jones explained. "The tough job is avoiding them."

Courage (See Traits, Valor)

313. What is more mortifying than to feel that you've missed the plum for want of courage to shake the tree?

—Logan P. Smith

314. Addressing a group of experts takes courage, like the father who had been putting off the discussion of sex with his boy. Finally, he mustered enough courage, called the boy into his den and said, "Son, I'd like to discuss with you some of the facts of life."

The boy said, "Father, that's fine. Now, what would you like to know?"

315. No man has more courage than the one who can stop after he has sampled one peanut from a bag.

316. Courage is grace under pressure.

—Ernest Hemingway

317. Courage is one product that never goes out of date.

318. Courage is taking a final examination after missing half the lectures.

319. In a recent newspaper, I came across an interesting article written by a high school senior. The young man carried a small card in his wallet and whenever he needed more courage, he read it.

Don't look, you might see.
Don't listen, you might hear.
Don't think, you might learn.

Don't walk, you might stumble.
Don't run, you might fall.
Don't live, you might die.

—Author Unknown

Courtesy (See Manners)

320.   Knowledge, ability, experience, are of little avail in reaching high success if courtesy be lacking. Courtesy is the one passport that will be accepted without question in every land, in every office, in every home, in every heart in the world. For nothing commends itself so well as kindness; and courtesy IS kindness.

—Good Reading

321.   Courtesy is a master key. It will unlock most any door, anywhere—in the store, along the traveler's road, and especially in the home. And those few doors courtesy will not unlock would not be worth entering anyway.

322.   Life is not so short, but there is always some time for courtesy.

—Emerson

323.   The small courtesies sweeten life; the greater, ennoble it.

—Bovee

Creative Workshop (See Conventions)

324.   Have you heard about the newest "creative workshop?" The subject is "Expense Accounts."

Criticism

325.   Criticism can be avoided by saying nothing, doing nothing and being nothing.

326.   Constructive criticism from a wise man is more to be desired than the enthusiastic approval of a fool.

327.   The mud slinger never has clean hands.

328.   Secretary to her school administrator: "I've taken all the criticism of my work that I'm going to take. How do you spell 'quit'?"

329.   A critic is a fellow who goes along for deride.

330.   Critics are people who go places and boo things.

331.   A school principal rushed to his attorney indignant over an article that appeared in the local paper severely criticizing the man. He wanted to know if he should demand a public apology or file suit for damages.

"I wouldn't do anything," the attorney advised. "Half the people who read the paper never saw the article. Half of those who saw it didn't understand it. Half of those who did understand it didn't believe it and half of those who did believe it are of no consequence anyway."

332.   I have yet to find a man, however exalted in his position, who did not do better work or put forth greater effort under a spirit of approval than under the spirit of criticism.

—Charles Schwab

333.   If criticism had any real power to harm, the skunk would be extinct by now.

—Fred Allen

D

Decisions

334.   An instructor's wife took her little son to the corner store

with her. The shopkeeper saw the boy look longingly at a tray of jelly beans in the candy case, so he pulled out the tray and told the boy to reach in and take a handful. The boy, however, merely shook his head.

"What's the matter, sonny?" asked the shopkeeper. "Don't you like jelly beans?"

"Yes, I do," murmured the child.

Whereupon the kindly man told the boy to hold out his cap and dropped a generous handful of candy into it.

Later, the mother asked the boy why he refused the storekeeper's offer to help himself.

The boy answered: "His hand was bigger 'n mine."

335.   If you have difficulty making decisions, don't eat at that place that has "28 flavors of ice cream."

Degree (Alumni, Diploma, Education, Graduation)

336.   "Many colleges are no longer giving Bachelor of Arts degrees. After four years you become a certified guerrilla fighter."

—Bob Hope
Family Weekly

337.   We've noticed something about college girls. Some of them go to college to win bachelors' degrees; others go to win bachelors BY degrees.

338.   A divinity student named Tweedle
Refused to accept his degree;
He didn't object to the Tweedle
But hated the "Tweedle D.D."

Determination (See Ambition, Trait)

339.   "It's not easy to get ahead in this world," a businessman told a college class. "As a lad I started out at the bottom. I worked, struggled, sweated, climbing the ladder of life, hand over hand, rung by rung."

"And now," asked a student, "you are a great success?"

"Well, no," admitted the businessman, "but I'm getting pretty darn good at climbing ladders."

Diploma (See Degree, Graduation Speaking)

340.   "Is that your college diploma you have framed there?"
"Well, it's sort of a diploma. It's a worthless stock certificate showing that I've been through the school of experience."

341.   The diploma you get from the School of Hard Knocks is not sheepskin—it's a piece of your own.

342.   Some high schools have withheld diplomas from bearded students even though their grades were excellent. It would be tough to do well in math, English and chemistry, and then flunk shaving.

Diplomacy (See Manners, Tact)

343.   "Dad," said the high school student, looking up from the book he was reading, "what is meant by 'diplomatic phraseology'?"
"Well," replied the father, "if you were to say to a homely girl 'Your face would stop a clock,' that would be stupidity. But if you said to her, 'When I look into your eyes, time stands still,' that would be diplomatic phraseology."

344.   A diplomat is a chap who, when asked what his favorite color is, replies "Plaid."

345.   Diplomacy is to do and say the nastiest thing in the nicest way.

346.   The real diplomat is a woman who can look happy when she has an unexpected dinner guest.

347.   A diplomat is a man who remembers a woman's birthday and forgets her age.

—The Crossett (Ark.) *News Observer*

348. Diplomacy is the art of saying "nice doggie" until you can find a rock.

—F.G. Kernan

Discipline (See Behavior, Punishment)

349. At the end of her patience, the mother threatened to spank her young son. The youngster immediately fled up the stairs and dived under a bed to escape the punishment.

When the father came home, the mother told him what had happened. He went upstairs to coax the boy out, and began crawling under the bed where the boy was hiding.

In an excited whisper the boy said, "Hello, Pop, is she after you again, too?"

—*Advertiser's Digest*

350. "Well, Tommy, I hear that you and Mike Smithers almost got into a fist fight in the hallway," said the principal cooly.

"Yessir, that wise guy," Tommy replied. "We would of really had a battle, only they wasn't nobody there who'd hold us apart."

351. Little Freddie: "Boy, today is the fifth day this week I've had to stay after school."

Little Tommy: "I'll bet you're glad it's Friday."

352. Strangely enough, spare the rod and you get a beat generation.

353. A friend of ours says he got so many spankings when he went to school that he can still go to a fortune teller and have his father's palm read.

—T. Liepke in Quote

354. "Why was the cannibal expelled from school?"

"He was caught buttering up one of his teachers."

Discontent (See Misfortune)

355.   In the destiny of every moral being there is an object more worthy of God than happiness—it is character. And the grand aim of man's creation is the development of a grand character—and a grand character is, by its very nature, the product of probationary discipline.

—Austin Phelps

356.   Young student (about to be spanked): "Dad, did grandpa spank you when you were little for doing something wrong?"

Father: "Yes, son."

Student: "And did grandpa's father spank him?"

Father: "Yes he did."

Student: "And did great-grandpa's father spank him, too?"

Father: "He surely did."

Student: "Well, don't you think it's about time to stop this inherited brutality?"

Discontent (See Misfortune)

357.   A story that has been making the rounds is about the girl who entered a very strict religious order. Members were permitted to speak only once every five years and then allowed to only say two words. At the end of the first five years the member appeared before the Superior and was granted permission to speak. She said, "Bed hard," and was dismissed.

Five years later she appeared and was permitted to speak. This time she said, "Food bad."

Another five years passed and she again appeared for permission to speak. This time she said, "I quit."

The Superior looked at her for a long time and finally said, "I expected this. You have done nothing but complain ever since you've been here."

Dramatics (See Plays, Theatre)

358.   A five-year-old boy had one line in a kindergarten Christmas pageant, appearing in an angel's garb to say: "I bring you good tidings!"

After a rehearsal the boy asked his mother what "tidings" were. She explained tidings were good news.

Came the performance and he became flustered. After a long, embarrassing silence, he blurted out: "Hey, I got news for you!"

359.   The cub reporter who was assigned to cover the class plays of the high school made the following obstetrical report:

"The auditorium was filled with expectant mothers, eagerly awaiting the appearance of their offspring."

360.   Teacher: "Can someone tell me the difference between drama and melodrama?"

Student: "In a drama the heroine merely throws the bad guy over. In a melodrama, she throws him over a cliff."

361.   Two students were discussing the class play. "All I can say about it," said one, "is that nobody booed the performers."

"How could they?" said the other. "How can you yawn and boo at the same time?"

Driving (See Automobiles)

362.   Nothing will improve driving like the discovery that your license has expired.

363.   A student was telling his mother about the ride with his father.

"Gee, Mom," he said, "we passed two idiots, three morons, four darn fools, and I don't know how many knotheads."

364.   Student Motorist: "What am I supposed to do with this receipt you gave me for paying my ticket?"

Officer: "Keep it. When you collect four of them you get a bicycle."

365.   The average child learns to walk when he is one year old, but forgets it, it seems, as soon as he gets a driver's license.

—Bob Boehm in the *Review*

366.   A teacher was nearly struck by a teenage driver as he was crossing the street from the school. The car screeched to a halt, but instead of

Driving (See Automobiles)

giving the student a tongue lashing he deserved, he merely pointed to a pair of baby shoes dangling from the rear view mirror in the car and said:

"Young man, why don't you put your shoes back on."

367.   The time of day when traffic moves at a snail's pace is ironically called "the rush hour."

368.   If you make a right turn from a left lane, you are probably just careless and reckless and not at all what the fellow behind you called you.

369..   Each year it takes less time to fly around the world and more time to drive to school.

370.   One of life's briefest moments is the time between reading the sign on the freeway and realizing you just missed the off-ramp.

371.   Officer to student driver: "Young lady, you were doing 70 miles an hour!"

Student: "Isn't that wonderful! I only learned to drive just yesterday."

372.   The professor and his wife arrived at the main highway. The husband prepared to make a turn into the expressway. "Look your way," he ordered. "Any cars coming?"

"No."

He started to make his turn when she added: "Only a truck."

373.   You can't fool all the people all the time, but those highway interchange signs come pretty close.

374.   Professor: "How long did it take *you* to teach your wife to drive?"

Colleague: "It'll be ten years this August."

Drop-outs (See High School Students, Juvenille Delinquents)

375. The trouble with school drop-outs is NOT that they can't see the handwriting on the wall, but that they can't read it.

376. The Illinois superintendent of schools introduced in the state legislature a bill to deny driver licenses to school dropouts under 18.

Drugs (See Tranquilizers)

377. With all the drugs and alcohol being consumed, this could be termed the Stoned Age.

—H.D. Martz in the *Wall Street Journal*

378. There was a time when you used to look in the dictionary to spell "marijuana." Now you look in the morning newspaper.

379. Remember when a *Trip* involved travel in cars, planes and ships?
When *Pot* was a vessel for cooking things in?
When *Hooked* was what Grandmother's rug might have been?
When *Grass* was a groundcover, normally green?
And the *Pill* might have been what you took for a cough?

E

Ecology (See Conservation, Education, Science)

380. You're an older teacher if you went to school when they taught that hydrogen and oxygen were the only two ingredients in water.

381. The only favorable thing to be said for polluted air is that it's better than no air at all.

382. If you think pollution is bad today, talk with an old timer who remembers black smoke pouring from factories and homes burning nothing but soft coal, black dirty grime left by coal-burning trains, muddy roads and unpaved streets, and when everyone burned leaves and trash ... even on laundry Monday.

383. Ashes to ashes and dust to dust,
If smog doesn't get you, then pesticides must.

384. The air pollution people have a new theme: "We'll be Overcome Some Day."

Economics (See Business Education)

385. Professor of Economics: "Give me an example of indirect taxation."
Freshman: "The dog tax, sir."
Professor: "How is that?"
Freshman: "The dog doesn't have to pay it."

386. What this country needs most is a good five-cent anything.
—Plough Hand

387. An economist is a person who knows more about money than the people who have it know.

388. If all the economists were placed end to end, they wouldn't reach a conclusion.
— The Tiro (O.) *World*

Education (See Absent-Minded, College, High School, Kindergarten, School, Self-Improvement, Students, Wisdom)

389. A little learning is a dangerous thing. Ask any child who has brought home a bad report card.

Education (See Absent-Minded, College, High School, Kindergarten, etc.)

390. You can lead a lad to school, but you can't make him think.

391. A youth who short changes his education now will probably be short of change the rest of his life.

392. A good education helps you worry about what's going on all over the world.

393. The important thing is not so much that every child should be taught as that every child should be given the wish to learn.
—John Lubbock

394. Student: "It says here that if we study hard, don't drink, smoke or run around with girls, we'll live longer. Is that true?"
Professor: "We don't know for sure. Somebody has to try it."

395. There was a time when aid to education meant Dad was helping Junior with his homework.

396. "To keep up your education," a college commencement speaker told a graduation class of men "sit down and read whenever your wives tell you they're ready to go out except for hat and gloves. You'll be amazed how much knowledge you'll acquire."

397. Education: The ability to describe fully a bathing beauty without using your hands.

398. Mary Wilson Little: "He who devotes 16 hours a day to hard study may be as wise at 60 as he thought himself at 20."

399. It is the studying that you do after your school days that really counts," noted H.L. Doherty. "Otherwise you know only that which everyone else knows."

400. Learning makes a man fit company for himself.
—Edw. Young

401. The only thing that's more expensive than education is ignorance.

402. Most of us seem to have come through the knowledge explosion without a scratch.

403. A well-known New York book publisher told us: "A book on Memory Training will not sell, because memory training makes you think. To think is to work. The mind doesn't want to work."

404. Thinking is very far from knowing.

—H.G. Bohn

405. Any parent will confirm that youngsters are at their mental peaks at age 4 and 17. At 4 they know all the questions. At age 17 they know all the answers.

406. Higher education has distinct advantages. You seldom see a misspelled picket sign on a campus.

407. The average guy who looks under a car's hood doesn't know any more about it than the guy who used to look in a horse's mouth.

408. To accuse others for one's own misfortunes is a sign of want of education; to accuse oneself shows that one's education has begun; to accuse neither oneself nor others shows that one's education is complete.

—Epictetus

409. If you think that our kids don't know the value of a dollar, just ask them how many gallons of gasoline it will buy.

—Don Radde

410. Education is an admirable thing, but it is well to remember from time to time that nothing that is worth knowing can be taught.

—Oscar Wilde

Education (See Absent-Minded, College, High School, Kindergarten, etc.)

411. When quizzed about her progress in a memory course, the young stenographer explained: "I never could remember what I was supposed to remember, but now I *can* remember that I forget to remember it."

412. If you make people think they're thinking, they'll love you. Really make them think and they'll hate you.

—Don Marquis

413. Harvard's famed Professor Charles T. Copeland was once asked by a student:

"Is there anything I can do to learn the art of conversation?"

"Yes, there is one thing," said Copeland. "If you will listen I will tell you."

For several moments there was silence. Then the student said, "I am listening professor."

"You see!" said Copeland. "You are learning already."

414. The problem of education is two-fold: first to know and then to utter. Everyone who lives any semblance of an inner life thinks more nobly and profoundly than he speaks.

—Robert Louis Stevenson

415. Chess is now an optional course for Mexican schoolboys. It's recommended for mental discipline.

416. The scientist had come back to his home town and was giving a lecture. "Now, I am sure that all of you know what a molecule is?" he said quizzically, gazing over his audience.

The chairman of the program committee, eager to show he was well-informed on all the latest technology (and wanting to see good rapport between speaker and audience), stood up and said smilingly:

"I'm sure most of us do, Doctor, but perhaps you'd better explain for the benefit of those who have never been up in one."

—*Atlanta Constitution*

417. One of our problems is that when people conclude their schoolwork they also conclude their skullwork.

418. They really shouldn't ban praying in public schools ... that's the only way most of us got through.

419. We don't know whether modern man has learned much, but he's certainly taut enough.

420. It's what you learn after you know it all that counts.

421. Bill: "Why did you spend so much money to learn speed-reading?"

Jack: "My boy, when you drive the expressways like I do, you read fast or you never get off."

422. There's only one corner of the universe you can be certain of improving and that's yourself.

—Aldous Huxley

423. Wife to reluctant husband who is helping their small son with his homework: "Help him now while you can. Next year he goes into the fourth grade."

424. I have learned silence from the talkative, toleration from the intolerant and kindness from the unkind.

—Kahlil Gibran

425. The other day little Timmy asked what the word "extinct" meant.

His teacher explained. "Suppose all life on earth was wiped out. Then you could say the human race was extinct."

Timmy thought for a moment, then asked. "Who would you say it to?"

—Ed Liska. *Chilton Times-Journal*

426. A man is educated who knows how to make a tool of every faculty—how to open it, how to keep it sharp, and how to apply it to all practical purposes.

—Henry Ward Beecher

427.   If your palm itches, it's a sign that you're going to get something. If your head itches, you've got it.

—*The Greybull* (Wy.) *Standard*

428.   Any child who gets raised by the book must be a first edition.

429.   Minds are like parachutes. They only function when they are open.

—Thomas Dewar

430.   Education is a handicap; it fills the mind with wrong notions before the opportunity comes to see the facts.

—Edward Welbourne

431.   Motto hanging on wall of research department office: "This problem when solved will be simple."

432.   A good deal of education is like the Indian Snake Dance. It doesn't bring rain, but makes the dancer feel better.

—*Phi Delta Kappan*

433.   He who is afraid of asking, is ashamed of learning.

434.   A student in a Bible study class was listening to a discussion of Dan and Beersheba, and it was obvious that he was becoming quite confused. Finally, he stood up and asked the teacher, "Pardon, sir, but am I to understand that Dan and Beersheba are the names of places?"

"Yes," said the teacher.

"Oh, dear," said the student, blushing with embarrassment. "All these years I've thought they were husband and wife like Sodom and Gomorrah."

435.   Train a child in the way he should go, and when he is grown he'll tell you how wrong you were.

—*Smiles*

436.   A youngster wrote to the Library of Congress: "I am no help to my teachers because I have no research information. I would appreciate it very much if you could send me anything about anything."

437.   Learning to be kind, tolerant and understanding is part of a liberal education even though not specifically taught in any classroom.

—Miami Herald

438.   Learn from the mistakes of others—you can't live long enough to make them all yourself.

439.   A twelve-year-old boy describes "mixed emotions": "It's like hearing the morning siren telling you that school is closed because of a blizzard—and you are in bed with the flu."

440.   Teacher: "What do you mean, calling an electric chair a piece of Period Furniture?"
Student: "Well, it ends in a sentence doesn't it?"

441.   "You can send a message around the world in less than a second, but it takes years to get it through the human skull."

—Charles F. Kettering

442.   Education replaces cocksure ignorance with thoughtful uncertainty.

443.   Some children's education has entirely cured their mothers of bragging about them.

444.   Good education helps you worry about what's going on all over the world.

445.   For the fellow who gets his education from the daily papers—if he should happen to miss one—he has lost all he is supposed to know for the next 24 hours.

446.   The roots of education are bitter, but the fruit is sweet.
                                              —Aristotle

447.   He who is taught to live upon little owes more to his father's wisdom than he who has a great deal felt him does to his father's care.

                                              —William Penn

448.   I have known countless people who were reservoirs of learning yet never had a thought.

                                              —Wilson Mizner

449.   Progressive education should mean the kind that advances directly from misdemeanor to punishment.
                    —Marcelene Cox in the *Ladies' Home Journal*

Egotism (See Traits)

450.   Ego is when a man sitting in a crowded bus flirts with a woman who is standing.

                                              —Extra

451.   Egotism is the anesthetic that dulls the pain of stupidity.
                                              —Frank Leahy

452.   Maybe it's a good thing you can't see yourself as others see you; you'd only get mad about it.

453.   Egotism is what enables a man who's in a rut to think he's in the groove.

454.   Egotist: a person who plays too big a part in his own life.

                                              —Dan Bennett

455. The human body is extremely sensitive . . . Pat a man on the back and his head swells.

456. We knew a man who was such an egotist that, on his birthdays, he always sent his mother a card of congratulations.

457. One of the hardest secrets for a man to keep is his opinion of himself.

English (See Grammar, Language, Spelling, Words)

458. A teacher wrote this sentence on the board and asked her class to correct it: Girls is naturally more beautiful than boys.
One little boy wrote: Girls is artificially more beautiful than boys.

459. Child: Mother, why is English called the "mother tongue?"
Mother: Because fathers get to use it so seldom.

460. "Why didn't you get one hundred in English?" asked the mother.
"I had the period upside down," explained her son.

461. The teacher asked her pupils to write a short composition, using "Water" as the subject. One small boy had considerable trouble with his effort, but this is what he wrote:
"Water is a white, wet liquid which turns black when you wash in it."

462. English Department: Chamber of Commas.

463. An African teacher flew to the United States to attend an international educational conference. He was met at the airport by his American host.
"Was your flight comfortable?" the host asked him.
The African exploded into a series of raucous noises: "screech, s-s-s-s-, whistle, z-z-z-z-, honk" and then in perfect English added, "Yes, it was most pleasant."
"And how long are you planning to stay in America?"

Once again the teacher preceded his remarks with the same noises as before and then answered, "For about two weeks."

The host, not wishing to comment on the unusual noises, asked, "Tell me, where did you learn such perfect English?"

After the same noisy preliminaries, he said, "Short-wave radio."

464. The teacher was discussing conjunctions with her young students. After explaining that conjunctions were words that connect other words in the sentence she asked for volunteers to give examples of conjunctions.

One little boy raised his hand and answered, "I now pronounce you man and wife."

465. Teacher: "Tell me, Jimmy, what it means when I say 'I love, you love, he loves.'"

Jimmy: "It means the movie ain't going to be a cowboy story."

466. Teacher: "Can someone in this class give me three collective nouns?"

Student: "Flypaper, wastebasket and vacuum cleaner."

467. The teacher explained to her class that a "collision" is when two things come together unexpectedly.

"Can someone give an example of a collision?" she asked.

"Yes," a little girl replied. "Twins."

468. There's the student who sent his English theme by freight because he couldn't express himself.

469. "Now, can anyone in the class give me a sentence with the word heterodology in it?"

Student: "NO!"

470. First student: "Great Scott! I've forgotten who wrote Ivanhoe!"

Second Student: "If you tell me who in the dickens wrote the 'Tale of Two Cities' I'll tell you."

Entomology (See Nature Study, Science)

    471.   Teacher: "Take this sentence, 'Let the cow be taken to the pasture.' What is the mood?"

Johnny: "Why the cow, of course!"

    472.   A student in the English class fell asleep as the teacher was reading one of the Canterbury Tales. Annoyed when he saw the student asleep, the professor let fly with the book, bouncing it off the sleeper's head.

"What hit me;" cried the victim.

"That," said the teacher, "was a flying Chaucer."

    473.   When asked to define the difference between a "bolt" and a "nut," a student replied that a "bolt is a thing like a stick of hard metal such as iron with a square chunk on one end and a lot of scratching wound on the other."

"A nut is similar to a bolt, only the opposite, being a hole in a little chunk of iron, sawed off short, with wrinkles around the inside of the hole."

Entomology (See Nature Study, Science)

    474.   The Wisconsin Agricultural Marketing Service, which keeps tabs on weather and crops via a network of field men, received this comment from an unidentified Marinette County observer:

"Large mosquitoes this year . . . saw one yesterday with four woodticks on it."

    475.   A teacher asked her pupils to write about some kind of insect they were familiar with.

One little girl decided to write about ants.

"My subject," she wrote "is about Ants. Ants are of two kinds, insects and lady uncles. Sometimes they live in holes and sometimes they live with their married sisters."

    476.   One firefly said to the other: "I feel so foolish. I've been talking to a cigarette butt for the past five minutes."

Evolution (See Heredity)

    477.   Two monkeys were discussing the theory of evolution: "Do you mean to tell me that I am my keeper's brother?"

478.   Evolution: Dress, $6.95; Gown, $45; Creation, $225.

Examinations (See Homework, School)

479.   "I'm convinced," complained the history professor to the football coach, "that your fullback, McRam, copied the exam answers on my last test from the paper of the bright fellow who sits beside him. The only two answers he had wrong were the same ones the good student had wrong."

"Could have been a coincidence," said the coach.

"Maybe so. But the scholar answered one question with 'I don't know,' and the same question on McRam's paper was answered, 'I don't know either.' "

—Nuggets

480.   Of 1,000 New Jersey college students polled on how to prevent classroom cheating, more than 21 percent offered this foolproof solution: To end cheating on exams, stop giving exams.

481.   Said the professor taking up the quiz papers, "Why are there quotation marks on this paper?"

"Well," answered the lazy student, "it's a courtesy to the man on my left."

482.   The final examination question was a real puzzler. It asked why "psychic" was spelled with a "P."

The young coed was having a hard time with the question. After thinking about it until the time was almost up, she finally, in desperation, wrote: "It pcertainly does pseem psilly."

483.   During a Christmas exam, one of the questions was "What causes a depression?" One of the students wrote: "God knows! I don't. Merry Christmas!"

The exam paper came back with the prof's notation: "God gets 100. You get zero. Happy New Year."

484.   One of the questions on a grade school test paper read: "In the fall why do wild geese fly south?"

In six words a schoolboy solved one of nature's mysteries that has baffled waterfowl experts since they were recognized experts. His answer was, "Because it's too far to walk."

485. Note on bottom of college exam paper: "I wasn't smart enough to look at anyone's paper and they were all too smart to look at mine."

486. As long as there are final exams, there will always be prayers in our schools.

487. Note on student's final examination paper: "I didn't get any help and my grade will prove I couldn't have given any."

488. 1st Student: "Did you pass trig?"
2nd Student: "No, I flunked. My teacher said I didn't know math from a hole in the ground."

489. This fellow studied five years to be a druggist and flunked the final test because he forgot to put a nut on the banana split.

490. An intelligence test sometimes shows a man how smart he'd have been not to have taken it.

491. An irate parent called his son's teacher to complain of the mark his son received in an examination.
"How dare you give my son an 'F' on his examination," the parent complained. "My son studied all night before the examination. He shouldn't have received such a mark."
"You're right," remarked the teacher. "And I'm sorry, but you see it was the lowest possible mark I could give."

492. Billy looked depressed and his mother asked him what was the matter.
"I got a test paper back and it was marked 'Excellent.' "
"Why that's wonderful," said his mother. "But why are you upset?"
"The paper is not mine."

Experience (See Age)

493. What a man knows at 50 that he did not know at 20 boils down to something like this: the knowledge that he has acquired with age is not the knowledge of formulas, or forms of words, but of people, places, actions—a knowledge not gained by words but by touch, sight, sound, victories, failures, sleeplessness, devotion, love—the human experiences and emotions of this earth; and perhaps, too, a little faith and a little reverence for the things you cannot see.

—Adlai Stevenson

494. Look here, what did you mean by telling me you had five years' experience when you've never even had a job before?

Young graduate: Well, you advertised for a man with imagination.

495. Broadmindedness has been defined as highmindedness flattened by experience.

—Atlantic Coast Line News

496. Only eyes washed by tears can see clearly.

—Dr. Louis L. Mann

497. Good judgment comes from experience, and experience comes from poor judgment.

498. Experience is not what happens to a man. It is what a man does with what happens to him.

—Aldous Huxley

499. Some people speak from experience and others, from experience, don't speak.

—Illinois Journal of Education

500. One reason experience is such a good teacher is that she doesn't allow dropouts.

Expert (See Consultant)

501. The reason the school of experience is so tough is that you get the test first and then you get the lesson.

502. A little experience often upsets a lot of theory.

503. The school of experience charges more for its night courses.

504. Experience is what you have when you are too old to get a job.

505. Experience teaches us too many darn things we don't want to learn.

Expert (See Consultant)

506. An expert is a man from out of town.
—Newspapermen's Saying

507. There are all kinds of "experts." A "microscopic expert," for example, is one who magnifies everything.

508. An expert is someone who takes some information that you already know and confuses it.

509. An expert is an ordinary teacher away from home.

Exploration (See Outer Space)

510. A famous university anthropoligist touring the jungles of central India came across a native village. "You people in the forest are certainly lost to civilization," he observed to the head man.

"We don't mind being lost," was the reply. "It's being discovered that worries us."

F

Faculty Meetings (See Meetings, Teachers)

511.　　Two elderly teachers ambled down the hall on their way to the weekly faculty meeting. The younger of the two broke the the silence. "Jim, why do you go to these meetings? Since your last serious heart attack, you know no one at school expects you to do anything but teach your classes, and your doctor has advised you to cut out all extracurricular activities because another attack might kill you. I know you've dropped all of your after-school clubs and you don't go to athletic events or PTA meetings any more, so why do you continue going to faculty meetings?"

"Frankly," the older teacher replied, "I'd welcome my last attack at one of these meetings. I can't think of any other place in this whole world where it would be easier to make the transition from life to death."

—Today's Education

Failure (See Examinations, Traits, Success)

512.　　There are five types of men who fail in life: the machine, the miser, the hermit, the snob and the brute.

—Walter Wilber Grube

513.　　Some of us are like a fence. We run around a lot without getting anywhere.

514.　　It takes very little effort to achieve failure.

515.　　There are two kinds of failures: Those who thought and never tried, and those who tried and never thought.

516.　　A failure is a man who is unable to cash in on his experiences.

517.　　When success turns a man's head, he is a failure.

Family Life (See Children Motherhood, Parenthood)

518. Lord Bulwer's life was a succession of failures, crowned with final triumph. His first novel was a *failure;* his first drama was a *failure;* so were his first speeches and poems. But he fought both defeat and ridicule and finally won a place with Thackeray and Dickens.

Family Life (See Children, Motherhood, Parenthood)

519. Money isn't everything, but it does keep you in touch with your children.

—Andy Jones, Waukesha

520. A first-grader was telling her teacher about her eight brothers and sisters.
"My," said the teacher, "a big family must be expensive."
"Oh no, we don't buy them, we raise them."

—Mrs. J. B. Ayers, Georgia

521. Nothing keeps the family together as much as owning just one car.

522. The old-fashioned family doctor is disappearing and so is the old-fashioned family.

523. Some teenagers regard home as a drive-in where pop pays for the hamburgers.

524. The teacher told his class when he was a boy on a farm they had a mule that was just like one of the family.
Student to his friend: "Yeah, and I know which one."

525. Teacher: "John, give me a definition of a home."
John: "A home is where part of the family waits until others are through with the car."

Fight (See Discipline, Military)

526. Samson used the jawbone of an ass to end a fight. These days that weapon is more often used to start one.

527.   Steel loses much of its value when it loses its temper.

528.   For several days a boy had been complaining that one of the children at school was picking on him. Deciding the time had come to teach his son something about the manly art of self-defense, the boy's father showed him how to make a fist and told him to let it fly the next time his playmate picked on him.

The next afternoon, the door burst open and the boy rushed in. His eyes were shining with triumph and excitement.

"Daddy," he shouted "I did it! I did it! I hit her!"

Flattery

529.   Flattery is often a gift-wrapped insult.

530.   If you say to a woman "How cool you look," she's pleased—but if you tell her she doesn't look so hot—wham!

531.   Flattery, as the fellow said, is the power to describe others as they see themselves.

Football (See Sports)

532.   There was a coach who was always exercising his football players' minds by asking them what they would do under such and such conditions during an important game.

Walking the sidelines one day, he stopped where Johnny was sitting and said, "Johnny, if it were third down and 25 yards to go, and we were on our own 45-yard line, what would you do?"

"I'd move to the other end of the bench so I could see the play better," said Johnny.

533.   The sports editor was interviewing a college coach. "What's your line-up for next season?" he asked.

"Well, I can't be sure at this point," was the reply, "but as of now it looks like this: Jackson, Lendowski and Watson will do the razor blade commercials; Hirsh, Smith and Taylor will go to deodorants; Russell and Stern will appear for shaving cream; and Samson is slated for breakfast cereals."

Football (See Sports)

534.   A high school football coach was often asked to referee other school games. Once, when officiating, he penalized a team fifteen yards. As he was pacing off the penalty the team's coach forgot control and screamed, "You stink!"

Instead of putting down the ball at the penalty point the referee paced off fifteen yards more, then shouted, "How do I smell from here?" No comment this time.

—J. Gustav White

535.   After experiencing his fifth loss of the season, the grumbling football coach of State High School addressed his team. "Most football games are lost somewhere between the defensive tackles," he shouted.

While he spoke, he noticed the defensive tackle about who he was speaking was catnapping in the back row.

"Hey Smith," he shouted, "where are most football games lost?"

Awaking with a start, Smith blinked and replied, "A lot of them are lost right here at State High, coach."

536.   The pollster must be like a football coach, ready with a lot of explanations if he is right, a lot of jokes if he is wrong.

537.   Though a deeply religious person, the football coach also was something of a realist. Before the big game against his rough, tough, traditional rival, he gathered his squad around him and warned them about the rough stuff the opponents would throw at them.

"Now fellers," he said, "The Good Book tells us that if an enemy smacks you on the cheek, that's all right. Turn your other cheek. And if the opponents smack that cheek too, it's still all right. But, gentlemen, the third lick—the third lick, I say belongs to you!"

538.   The football coach of a small college was trying to explain his team's disastrous season to a local newspaper reporter. "My biggest problem with this year's squad was that most of my boys were just too young and un-coordinated."

As the reporter remained silent the coach added desperately, "Why, as a matter of fact, one of my kids on the first string was so un-coordinated that he couldn't walk and chew gum at the same time!"

539.   Comment from a frustrated football coach after watching his inept team work out the last time prior to the opening game: "I wouldn't even let my mother-in-law run behind that line!

540.   The team was behind and the coach saw that the only thing that might pull it out of the fire for his team was sending in Mike, the player who was big on brawn and short on brains. Before sending him in, however, the coach decided to give him a pep talk.

"We gotta win this game, Mike," said the coach. "It's important, and it looks bad for us right now. The other team has outpassed, outrun and outkicked us all the way. The only way we can win is to scare the other team. So you get out there on the field and get ferocious, vindictive and fierce."

"Right, Coach," answered Mike, "just tell me what their numbers are."

541.   Coach: "What's his name?"
Manager: "Szachzhwerskinoplinitz"
Coach: "Good. Put him on the first string. I'll get even with those sports writers."

542.   Visitor: "Can you tell me the name of this school?"
Young man: "Sorry, mister, I'm just a football player here."

543.   Doctor: "Was it while you were on the football team that you were hurt?"
Steven: "No sir. It was when the football team was on me."
—Junior Life

544.   College Football Coach: "When I retire I want to be a warden of a penitentiary so the alumni won't come back to visit."

Fortuity

545.   Good fortune is as unpredictable as moving the garden hose . . . you may get a lot or suffer from inattention.

546.   Latest fortune-cookie message: "You will meet a cute brunette. You will give her money. She is our cashier."

547.   Hard work is the accumulating of easy things you didn't do when you should have.

Fraternity (See College, Students)

548.   The father, passing through his son's college town late one evening, thought he would pay his son a surprise visit. Arriving at the son's fraternity house, he rapped on the door but was unable to rouse anybody. Then from a second floor window came a sleepy voice.

"Whaddyah want?"

"Does Charlie Jones live here?" asked the father.

"Yeah," replied the voice, "bring him in."

549.   A fraternity house sent its curtains to be laundered. On the second day after the "Unveiling" a note was received from the sorority house across the street:

"Dear Sirs: May we suggest that you procure curtains for your windows? We do not care for a course in anatomy!"

The prompt answer read: "Dear Girls: May we remind you that the course you mention is entirely optional?"

550.   A fraternity man is a college student who doesn't have to buy his own clothes.

Friendship (See Love)

551.   In the pleasant pastime of browsing through the dictionary for word origins, there are many delightful little surprises—such as the discovery that the word "friend" evolved from old European words (freond, vriend, frijonds) meaning "love." This little fact is appropriate, we think, and it reminds us that the word "friend" is a special word, being based on that greatest of human feelings. Therefore, we should be more selective than we usually are, and refrain from loosely throwing the word "friend" around when we mean "acquaintance" or "associate."

552.   Acquaintance is a degree of friendship called slight when its object is poor or obscure, and intimate when he is rich or famous.

—Ambrose Bierce

553.   If you make a person like himself a little better you've made a good friend.

554.   One cynic defined friends as "two women who are mad at the same person."

555.   If you think it hard to meet new people, you should pick up the wrong golf ball.

556.   The man, whose ambitions had caused all Europe to tremble under the tread of marching feet, who had married a proud princess, and who had dictated terms to emperors, lived out his last years without a friend. The people of St. Helena looked at Napoleon with pity and distrust, even hatred; they did not befriend him. All his friends and consorts had deserted him when his fortunes changed and he went into exile.

When he died, there was not even a small monument erected to him on St. Helena. The garden in which he had walked lonely and brooding became a potato patch; the room in which he had played billiards became a hay-mow, and the room in which he died became a stable.

How could the most powerful man in Europe have become a man absolutely alone?

Probably the answer lied in the fact that Napoleon was not a man who believed in the friendship of men. Several times he had stated: "I care only for people who are useful to me, and so long as they are useful." And once he said: "I have tried to make courtiers; I have never pretended to make friends."

How else but alone, then, is a man going to end up if these are his feelings toward friendship?

Friendship is gained only by friendship. If you do not believe in giving your heart, you will never be given another's. If you have power or wealth, you might attract opportunists as a candle flame attracts moths—but as anyone knows, candle flames and moths do not make long-standing friendships with each other.

—Nuggets

557.   Be interested. Don't try to be interesting.
Be pleasing. Don't expect to be pleased.
Be entertaining. Don't wait to be entertained.
Be lovable. Don't wait to be loved.
Be helpful. Don't ask to be helped.

558.   You have to offer friendship first to make friendship last.
—Bill Copland

559.   Every time you lend money to a friend you damage his memory.

560.   Money may not buy friends but it surely helps a lot in entertaining them.

561.   A friend is someone you know all about, but whom you love anyway.

G

Generation Gap (See Adolescence, Age, Middle Age, Teenagers, Youth)

562.   There's only one thing wrong with the younger generation—a lot of teachers don't belong to it anymore.

563.   What do you tell your students when they ask what you looked at when you used to listen to the radio at night?

564.   The "generation gap" is what keeps World War II teachers from being able to get into their uniforms.

565.   The older we get the farther we had to walk to school in our youth.

566.   One nice thing about growing older is that you and your children can be on the same side of the generation gap.

Genius (See Ability, Wisdom)

567.   A genius is a man who shoots at something no one else can see, and hits it.

568.   A genius is a fellow who has the ability to avoid work by doing it right the first time.

Geography (See Education, Science, Students, Teachers)

569. Teacher, in geography class: "Where is the capital of the United States?"

Junior: "All over the world."

570. "Now can anybody tell me," asked the geography teacher, "where we find mangoes?"

"Yes Miss," replied a knowing little boy, "wherever woman goes."

571. Teacher: What are the people from XYZ noted for?

Student: Stupidity.

Teacher: Where did you ever get that idea?

Student: My book says their population is very dense.

572. Teacher: Where is the English Channel?

Student: I wouldn't know. We can't get it on our set.

573. Teacher: "Mike, where is Brazil?"

Mike (stalling): "Where do you think it is?"

Teacher: "I don't know."

Mike: "I don't think I know either."

574. "Now that we know that the earth is round," said the teacher. "Tell me, Thomas, would it be possible for you to walk around the earth?"

"No, sir," replied Thomas.

"And why not?"

"Because," was the unexpected reply, "I twisted my ankle sliding into second."

575. Teacher: "What are the principal products of Cuba?"

Student: "I don't know."

Teacher: "Where did we used to get our sugar?"

Student: "We always borrowed ours from our neighbors."

576. One of the first things that a man notices in a backward nation is that children there are still obeying their parents.

577.   If it's such a small world, why does it cost so much to run it?

578.   The world owes us nothing. It was here first.

579.   A youngster couldn't understand why the Mississippi River was called "The Father of the Waters."

"If it's the Father of the Waters," he said "it should be called Mr. Sippi—not Mrs. Sippi."

580.   It is a heartwarming moment when travelling geography teachers find something in common with other teachers, such as they grew up in the same zip code.

Government (See America)

581.   The class was writing a composition. One little boy, who wanted $100 very badly, wrote a personal letter to God, asking for it. His teacher, reading, it, decided to try to get it for him by sending the request to the White House.

The President acknowledge the boy's request with a check for $5.00.

Delighted at having received at least a partial answer to his written prayer, the boy wrote a thank-you note to God.

"P.S." he added. "I see You routed the money through Washington and they deducted their usual 95 per cent."

582.   A teacher wanted to buy some timber from a mountain landowner, but the owner was asking the top dollar and refused to lower his price.

"Why I can buy timber from the government cheaper than that," the teacher protested.

"Maybe so," agreed the mountaineer. "But th' guvment's in debt and I ain't."

583.   This IS a Democratic Country—the only place where you can say what you think without thinking.

584.   Democracy is the recurrent suspicion that more than half of the people are right more than half the time. It is the feeling of privacy in the voting booth, the feeling of communion in the libraries, the feeling of vitality everywhere. Democracy is a letter to the editor. Democracy is the score at the beginning of the ninth.

585.   Federal aid to education should start with teaching arithmetic in Washington.

586.   Federal aid is like giving yourself a transfusion by drawing blood from your right arm, returning it to your left, and spilling 80 per cent of it on the way across.

587.   Standing in line at the teller's window, I noticed one of our retired teachers handing the cashier a computer perforated check which was neatly and heavily creased down the middle.

The teller gently unfolded the check and began counting out currency. "You know," she said, "the Government doesn't like you to fold these checks."

Without hesitation, the old gentleman pocketed his money and snapped, "The Government does a lot of things I don't like either."

588.   Teacher: "Why does Uncle Sam wear such a tall hat?"
Senior: "It comes in handy when he passes it around."

589.   Years ago our pioneer forefathers went out and built an empire without interference. Today you have to get a permit to add a garage.

590.   What this country needs is fewer people who know what this country needs.

591.   "One thing we need in these United States," said the teacher in economics, "is a cheaper way to make history."

Graduation (See Alumni, College, Degrees, Diploma, Education, High School)

592.   Now is the time when college graduates learn that you can't get rich by degrees.

—Maurice Seitter

593.   Son: "Dad, instead of buying me an expensive graduation gift, why not give me something you've made yourself?"

Dad: "What's that?"

Son: "Money."

594.   The University president was delivering his baccalaureate speech. In the audience were an elderly couple, obviously foreigners, who were having difficulty understanding the address to the class.

"What he say?" the woman asked.

"Who?" asked her husband.

"The beeg fela in black robes. What he say?"

"He say, 'School is out!' "

595.   Lawyer to prospective client: "If you're not in serious trouble, I'll take the case. If you are in a jam and want to get out of it, my partner will handle it. If, on the other hand, you're involved and want to get in trouble, my son, who graduated from law school last week, will take it."

596.   "I think my son would look a little more natural if he stood with his hand out," the father said when he was being photographed with his son for a college graduation photo.

597.   What many college graduates miss when they go looking for a job is the cheerleader.

Grammar (See Education, English, Literature, Words, Writing)

598.   A university professor about to enter the men's room was shocked to see a respected colleague putting a pencil in his pocket as he emerged. "Good heavens!" he exclaimed. "Are you one of those who write on toilet walls?"

"Oh, no," answered the other. "I was just correcting the grammar."

599.   The college professor was trying to teach one of his students to use the correct grammar. The student wasn't too eager to learn, however.

"What difference does it make if I say 'bad' or 'badly'?" he asked. "They both mean the same thing."

The professor pointed to a shapely girl who had just passed by and said:

"My boy, look at that girl and tell me, are you looking at her stern or sternly?"

600.   Teacher: "Carol, can you use these words in a sentence: defeat, deduct, defense and detail?"

Carol: "Defeat of deduct went over defense before detail."

601.   Teacher: Name a collective noun.

Student: Garbage truck.

602.   To keep in practice, my former English teacher and her husband, also a teacher, have a running contest to detect each other's grammatical errors. The loser each week buys dinner out for both on Sunday.

I was visiting them one Saturday evening when neither had been able to detect an error for two weeks. The phone rang and the wife got up to answer it. In a moment she turned to us and exclaimed, "My sister just gave birth to a PAIR OF TWINS! What do you think of that?"

"Redundant!" cried her husband triumphantly.

—Allen Smajstral (Victoria, Texas)

603.   The grammar teacher asked her pupils to supply antonyms for certain words. "What is the opposite of sorrow?" she asked.

"Joy," was the quick response.

"That's correct. Now what is the opposite of misery?"

"Happiness," called out one student.

"Right, Now give me the opposite of woe."

"Giddy-ap!" came a voice from the rear.

604.   Teacher: "I have went. That is wrong, isn't it?"

Pupil: "Yes ma'am."

Teacher: "Why is it wrong?"

Pupil: "Because you ain't went yet."

605.   Everybody knows that money talks, but nobody notices what kind of grammar it uses.

606.   Synonym is the word you use when you can't spell the word you want to use.

Habits (Trait)

607.   Lady of the house: "I don't need none."
Salesman: "How do you know? I might be selling grammar books."

608.   No, no, 'Lil Linda—spunk isn't the past participle of spank.

609.   The pupil was asked to paraphrase the sentence: "He was bent on seeing her."
This is what the pupil handed to the teacher: "The sight of her doubled him up."

610.   The king-size preposition-ending sentence was coined by the sick child who complained to his mother: "Why did you bring that book that I didn't want to be read to out of up for."

H

Habits (Trait)

611.   If there's anything harder than breaking a bad habit, it's trying to refrain from telling folks how you did it.

612.   Sunday comics are more habit forming than potato chips, says *Puck*.
But they're not as fattening.

613.   A habit cannot be tossed out of the window; it must be coaxed down the stairs a step at a time.

—Mark Twain

614.   The worst habit you can have is that of self pity.

615.   The real object of education is to give children resources that will endure as long as life endures; habits that time will ameliorate, not destroy; occupations that will render sickness tolerable, solitude pleasant, age venerable, life more dignified and useful, and death less terrible.

—Sidney Smith

616. The best way to stop a bad habit is never to start it.

—J.C. Penney

617. Habits are like popcorn. Once you've started, you don't want to stop.

Happiness (See Friendship, Love)

618. Happiness is when the noisy pump in your school aquarium quiets down and you keep from shouting to students on the other side of the room.

619. No one is born happy, but all of us are born with the ability to create happiness. A laugh expresses the joy of living and the person who laughs is a delight to be with. But more important—he is enjoying his own life.

—Master Barbers' Bulletin

620. One reason so many young students are always so happy is that they don't have kids of their own to worry about.

—Ties

621. Happiness is not having what you want, but wanting what you have.

—Hyman Schachtel

622. Nothing on earth can smile, but man. Flowers cannot smile; this is a charm that even they cannot calim. It is a prerogative of mankind; it is the color which love wears and cheerfulness and joy—these three. It is a light in the windows of the face, by which the heart signifies it is at home and waiting. It costs nothing but creates much. It enriches those who receive without impoverishing those who give. It happens in a flash and the memory of it sometimes lasts forever. None are so poor that they are not richer for its benefits. It creates happiness in the home and fosters good will in business. Yet it cannot be bought, begged, borrowed or stolen. It is something that is no earthly good to anybody till it is given away. If at times you meet someone who fails to give you a smile, may I ask that you give one of your own? For nobody needs a smile so much as those who have none to give.

623. Happiness to a teacher is not setting the alarm clock on Saturday night.

624. There is no duty we underrate so much as the duty of being happy.

—Robert Louis Stevenson

625. The days that make us happy make us wise.

—John Masefield

Hardship (See History)

626. Roughing it today is staying at a motel with a black and white set.

Health (See Medicine)

627. Ulcers are something you get from mountain-climbing over molehills.

628. "I am afraid, doctor, that the professor has some terrible affliction. Sometimes at home I talk to him for hours and then discover that he hasn't heard a word."

"That's not an affliction, Madam," he replied. "Your husband has a gift."

629. The trouble with people who enjoy ill health—they don't enjoy it alone.

—*Crawford County Independent*

630. They call the sick person a "patient" because that's what you have to be to get in to see a doctor these days.

631.   Doctors may prescribe sedatives, but not sleep; tranquilizers but not confidence; calmness, or happiness. Relaxation, mental normality must come from within; it is a quality man must develop himself.

—Advertiser's Digest

632.   Many teachers who say they're fit as a fiddle look more like a bass drum.

633.   The secret of good health is to leave the table hungry, the bed sleepy, and the tavern thirsty.

—Sidney Brody

634.   Health is what people drink to until they collapse.

—Angus Topics

635.   Health note: mixed greens are good for you, especially those tens and twenties.

—PTM Magazine

636.   Most people are quite happy to suffer in silence, if they are sure everybody knows they are doing it.

637.   A school teacher we know is such a devoted follower of the local newspaper Health column that she is worried that some day she will die of a misprint.

638.   Teachers don't get ulcers from what they eat, but from what's eating them.

639.   Students would be in better shape if they retained as much of what they read as what they eat.

Heredity (See Family Life)

640.   I never believed in heredity until two of my grandsons got all A's on their report cards.

641. During the great flood, Noah's Ark sprang a leak and Noah told his dog to put his nose against the hole. The water continued to rush in, so Noah asked his wife to stand over the spot. As the leak grew, Noah himself sat on the hole. And to this day, a dog's nose is always cold, a woman's feet are always clammy—and men always stand with their backs to the fireplace.

642. Heredity is what makes the mother and father of teenagers wonder a little about each other.

643. Medical men have about concluded that wrinkles are hereditary—from school children.

High School (See College, Diploma, Education, Examinations, Homework, Students, Teachers)

644. Pity the poor high school kids! Lots of them have to walk nearly as far to their parked cars as we used to walk to school.

—Memphis Commercial Appeal

645. "I'm sorry, son," said the father. "I have to use the car tomorrow to go out of town on business."

"But, Dad," complained the high school student. "How am I supposed to get to school?"

"Every kid in America gets to school! And you'll get to school like everyone else," replied the father. "You'll take the school bus."

History (See Military, Student, Sunday School)

646. Teacher: "Name one important thing we didn't have 50 years ago."

Gary J.: "Me!"

647. Ann, in school: "I wish I'd lived a thousand years ago."

Kate: "For goodness' sakes, why?"

Ann: "Think of all the history I wouldn't have to learn."

648.   After you've heard two eyewitness accounts of the same motor accident, you begin to worry about history.

649.   The major disaster in history was the invention of the wheel.

650.   Our pioneer forefathers were courageous, but they didn't have to live in constant fear of a power failure.

651.   History is being made faster than we can afford it.

652.   Sunday School teacher: "What lesson do we learn from the story of Jonah and the Whale?"
Pupil: "People make whales sick."

653.   Fifth-grade pupils were required to fill in the blanks in sentences on a history test. One of the sentences states: "The Declaration of Independence was written chiefly by . . ."
Neatly written in the blank space on test paper was the word "candlelight."

654.   During our study of the pioneer days in Michigan's history, my class discussed the fact that pioneers didn't have electricity or running water as we have today. I asked what they would do if they lived in pioneer days and didn't have running water. One pupil promptly answered, "I would call the board of water and light and have them come out and fix it!"
                                        —Paula Thomas, Lansing, Mich.

655.   One Sunday morning a group of children in a Pasadena Sunday School class was asked this seeming run-of-the-mill question: "Why did the Pilgrims invite the Indians to the very first Thanksgiving dinner?"
    "Because," said one straight-forward thinker, "There wasn't anybody else to invite."

115

656.　　　Teacher: "Johnny, what did George Washington say before crossing the Delaware?"

Johnny: "Get in the boat men."

657.　　　In a class of Greek history a youth was asked to tell the story of the battle of Thermopylae.

The lad had unusual descriptive ability and proceeded with great zest. No detail was left out. The heroic stand was described vividly. "—and they fought and fought and fought," said the pupil. "They fought until they lost their arms. Then they used their hands."

658.　　　Teacher (to History student): "You want to know why you didn't pass the history test? Well, your answer to the question 'Why did the pioneers go into the wilderness' was interesting from the standpoint of sanitation, but it was still incorrect."

659.　　　A teacher asked her first grade class how Noah spent his time on the Ark. As there was no response from the class, she added:

"Do you suppose he did a lot of fishing?"

"What?" responded one little 6-year-old, "with only 2 worms?"

660.　　　One reason history repeats itself is that so many people weren't listening the first time.

661.　　　We don't fully realize the hardships of our pioneers until we remember that day after day they plodded their way Westward into the setting sun WITHOUT sunglasses.

662.　　　History repeats itself so often it must be stuttering.

663.　　　Teacher: "What is the difference between a primitive and a modern man?"

Johnny: "When a wife talks too much a modern man goes to his club. A primitive man just reached for it."

664.　　　A Columbus boy was doing his homework and asked his father, "Dad, what's a Grecian urn?"

"I dunno," replied dad. "It probably depends on what he does."
—Bob Stanley, in the
Columbus Journal-Republican

665.   Remember back when a capsule traveled inside a man?

666.   Every line of history inspires a confidence that we shall not go far wrong; that things mend.
—Ralph Waldo Emerson

667.   Teacher: "What happened in 1492?"
Tenement Kid: "Don't ask me. We live in the basement."

668.   On George Washington's birthday, one teacher asked her class of youngsters if they knew what was the greatest difficulty Washington faced.
The Class was silent for a few minutes, and then one little boy answered, "He couldn't tell a lie."

669.   One of the reasons Cousin Woodrow failed his history test was because everything they asked him happened before the little fellow was born.

670.   You can't beat old Christopher Columbus' mileage. Look at all the miles he got out of three galleons.

671.   A ninth grade teacher asked her class in American history what might be the reaction of Henry Hudson if he returned now and sailed up the river that bears his name.
One student wrote: "He'd hold his nose and say, 'Phew!' "

672.   A teacher was discussing great men and women of our country during her fifth grade class when one girl began talking about two famous men who were the first to fly an airplane.
"Their names," she said, "were the Righteous Brothers."

673.   "Tommy, who was it who said, 'Give me liberty or give me death'?"

"Patrick Henry."

"That's right. Now who was it who said, 'I have come to bury Caesar, not to praise him'?"

"The undertaker."

674.   Teacher: "Can someone tell me when Rome was built?"
Student: "It was built during the night."
Teacher: "The night? Where did you ever get that idea?"
Student: "Well, everyone knows that Rome wasn't built in a day."

George Sato in *Boy's Life*

675.   "If George Washington were alive today, why couldn't he throw a silver dollar across the Potomac River?"

"Because a dollar doesn't go as far today as it used to."

676.   Teacher: "What did the Puritans come to this country for?"
Student: "To worship in their own way and make other people do the same."

677.   The history teacher was talking to a group of high school students about the old West. He remarked that Billy the Kid had killed 21 men by the time he was 21 years old.

"Good heavens!" exclaimed one of his students. "What kind of car did *he* drive?"

678.   Two high school students went into a museum where there was a mummy with a sign that read:243 B.C.
One student asked the other: "What does that mean?"
The other replied: "That's the license number of the car that hit him."

—Steve Sworen
Boy's Life

679.   Teacher: "Why did George Washington stand up in the boat?"
Student: "Because he was afraid someone would hand him an oar."

118

680. "Who discovered America?"

"Who do *you* think?"

"I don't think, I *know!*"

"I don't think I know, either."

681. History Teacher: "Today is a special historical anniversary. It was on this date that Pearl Harbor was attacked. Did you know that, Margaret?"

Margaret: "No, I didn't hear about Pearl Harbor. Who was she?"

682. It is much more difficult to talk about a thing than to do it. Anybody can make history. Only a great man can write it.

—Oscar Wilde

Hobbies

683. Hobby: Something you go goofy about to keep from going nuts about things in general.

684. Smugly surveying his stamp collection, his rock collection, his old gun collection, and his coin collection, the professor caught his wife by the arm as she hurried past with a mop in one hand and a bundle of dirty clothes in the other, and told her, "Mary, you don't know what you're missing, not having a hobby."

"Oh, I have a hobby, though," she said, blowing a wayward strand of hair away from her face, "I spend quite a bit of time trying to collect MYSELF."

685. Drudgery: Working like a dog for money.

Hobby: Doing it for nothing.

686. A hobby is something a person enjoys doing that is none of his business.

Home Economics—Cooking (See Lunch)

687. Home Economics Teacher: "When the sauce begins to boil, put in a tablespoonful of water."

Student: "Level or heaping?"

688.   Student: "I understand you dropped 'home economics.' How come?"

Other Student: "Too much work. Every recipe started the same way—'take a clean dish.' I'm not going to do dirty dishes all my life."

689.   Lulu is going to cooking school at night. Right now she's studying Advanced Defrosting.

690.   Heard about the new recipe for a sponge cake? You borrow all the ingredients.

—*Today's Chuckle*

691.   For one of her first dinners, a teacher's bride served "clove-studded baked ham" with the ends cut off. When her husband asked the reason for the cut ends, she explained: "Well, that's the way Mother always did it."

The next time his mother-in-law came over, he inquired about the cut ends, and she said "Why? Because that's the way my mother always did it."

When Grandma arrived for dinner one Sunday, she, too, was asked whether she sliced the ends off the ham. "Certainly," she said, "that's the only way I could get it in the pan."

—John Shotwell

Homework (See Examinations, Students, Teachers)

692.   TV programs got pretty dull this Fall. The children were doing their homework.

693.   A teacher advises that his high school students would do much better in their school work if their parents would pull a few wires. For a start, he recommends those attached to the telephone, ignition, radio, and television set.

694.   When we were in school, we did our homework on the dining room table. Nowadays, children all have scientifically-designed desks, which they lie next to while studying on the floor.

—*The Adams Country Times-Reporter*

695. Teacher: "I don't know how one person can make so many mistakes on his homework."

Pupil: "It wasn't one person. My father helped me."

696. Father: I'll help you with your arithmetic, Son. Now if I had 10 oranges and gave you 2 of them, how many oranges would I have left?

Son: I don't know. At school we do all our problems with apples.

—Helen L. Harrison, Tennessee

697. One parent mentioned the other day that with all the emphasis on sex education he was a little leary when his son casually remarked he was going over to help one of his classmates with her homework.

—*The Marion Advertiser*

698. The familiar picture of Abraham Lincoln studying by the light of an open fire can hardly be compared to the modern American youth doing his homework by the flickering light of his television set.

699. One parent to another: "After you've done homework for six kids, don't you wish you had loved and lost?"

700. "That lump on the side of my brother's head," remarked the little girl to her teacher "is where Daddy helped with his homework."

701. A student was being reprimanded by his father for his low grades in school.

"Well, all the boys at school got C's and D's, too," he said.

"All of them?" questioned his father. "How about little Jimmy who lives down the street?"

"Oh, he got high grades," the youngster admitted. "But he's different. His parents are able to help him with his homework."

Humor—Sense of (See Happiness, Introductions)

702. The professor stepped up on the platform and by way of breaking the ice, he remarked, "I've just been asked to come up here and say something funny."

At this point, a student heckler in the back of the hall called out, "You'll tell us when you say it, won't you?"

The professor answered, "I'll tell you—the others will know."

703. A smile is a gentle curved line that sets a lot of things straight.

704. A sense of humor is what makes you laugh at something you'd get mad at if it happened to you.

705. A sense of humor is a man's best armor against life's daily frustration.

706. A student in the next chair remarked that the lecturing professor was so boring that he almost fell asleep. "What he needs are some good gags," he remarked.

"How about an old towel?"

707. Men show their characters in nothing more clearly than what they think laughable.

—Goethe

708. You cannot laugh at anything unless you have mastered your anxieties about it.

I

Ideas

709. An idea is more than information; it is information with legs on it.

—Edgar Dale

710.   There are some people who think that an idea is to be rated like wine: the older, the better. The resort to antiquity's cellar may yield vinegar as often as it produces wine.
—Aaron Levenstein, *"Use Your Head"*

711.   Plenty of people can get an idea. The point is to find an idea that gets plenty of people.

712.   Ideas are like children—your own are wonderful.
—John Kirkpatrick
Waupun Leader-News

713.   Ideas are strange; they never work unless you do.

Ignorance (See Wisdom)

714.   If it is true that "ignorance is bliss," why is there so much unhappiness?

715.   Ignorance is when you don't know anything and somebody finds it out.

Income (See Cost of Living)

716.   Income: An amount of money—large or small—which you spend more than.
—The Milton (Ontario) Canadian Champion

717.   Living on a small teacher's income wouldn't be so hard to do if it weren't for the effort to keep it a secret.
—*The Indianapolis Star*

718.   Your friends don't believe you make as much as you say you do. The government doesn't think you make as little.

Intellectural (See Genius, Wisdom)

719.　　Income seems to be something you can't live without—or within.

720.　　People who live within their incomes are just messing up the economy.

721.　　What constitutes a living wage depends upon whether you are giving it or getting it.

Intellectual (See Genius, Wisdom)

722.　　An intellectual is a person who can listen to the "William Tell Overture" without thinking of the Lone Ranger.

Introductions

723.　　Al Capp, creator of Li'l Abner, was hustled by a Washington hostess during a cocktail party to meet an important guest. She said to the guest, "Mr. President, I'd like you to meet the famous comic strip cartoonist, Al Capp." The President asked, "What comic strip?" She then turned to Capp and said, "I'd like to introduce our President." Capp asked, "What country?"

724.　　Adam is the one man in the world who couldn't say, "Pardon me, but haven't I seen you some place before?"

725.　　The President of the Board of Regents of the University of Wisconsin was being introduced as the speaker of a local Kiwanis club. He was also a graduate from the University of Wisconsin.

"When Ken was going to the university," the toastmaster said when introducing him "his father didn't have much respect for his ability. No matter what Ken did his father gave him little encouragement.

"Ken was determined, however, to show his father that he had what it takes to make a success in college, so when he went off to Madison and at the University of Wisconsin he burned the midnight oil and excelled in his classes. When the semester was over he came out with a 90 average which he proudly showed his Dad.

"This didn't make much of an impression on his father and he only 'humphed' when Ken showed him his semester grades from Wisconsin.

"This made Ken furious. He felt more determined than ever to surpass his excellent grade the first semester and when the end of the first year rolled around, there was Ken right on the top of the freshman class.

"Ken thought this would surely change his father's opinion of his ability, so he proudly walked into his father's study with his record for the year and a letter from the Dean of his outstanding achievement.

"His Dad put on his glasses, looked over his grades and the letter from the Dean, and then turned to Ken and said:

"This doesn't say much for the University of Wisconsin."

Intuition

726.   Intuition is what enables a woman to contradict her husband before he says anything.

727.   Intuition is that unknown second sense that tells a woman that she is absolutely right, whether she is or not.

728.   Woman's Intuition: Suspicion that clicked.

729.   What passes for woman's intuition is often nothing more than man's transparency.

—George Jean Nathan

Inventions

730.   Little Boy: "Teacher, did Thomas Edison make the first talking machine?"
Teacher: "No, John. The Creator performed that feat in the Garden of Eden but Mr. Edison made the first one that could be shut off."

731.   Ben Franklin discovered electricity, but the person that invented the meter made the money.

732.   Teacher: "Who was Alexander Graham Bell?"
Student: "He was the first ding-a-ling."

Irony

733. High heeled shoes were invented by a woman who was always being kissed on the forehead.

Irony

734. Irony: a student giving his father a billfold for Christmas.

J

Journalism (See Word, Writing)

735. A team of student journalists recently toured a capital city, asking what the residents thought was the most important thing in the world. They got the answer: "Minding your own business."

736. Advice to J-School lads
From the working grads:
They don't pay cash
For poor trite trash.

    —Jim Wynn, *Editor & Publisher*

737. Student: "Do you think I should put more fire into my articles?"
Journalism Instructor: "No, vice versa."

738. Editor: "Did you write this poem yourself?"
Student Contributor: "Yes, every word of it."
Editor: "I'm certainly glad to meet you, Edgar Allan Poe. We thought you died a long time ago."

Juvenile Delinquents (See Adolescents, Teenagers, Youth)

739. A juvenile delinquent gets on the wrong track because of a misplaced switch.

740. Don't worry too much about the younger generation. Eventually, they'll slow down like the rest of us.

741.   Definition: Juvenile Delinquent—Child hood.

742.   The good old days were when a juvenile delinquent was a boy who played the saxophone too loud next door.

743.   Juvenile delinquents are other people's children.

744.   Delinquent children are those who have reached the age where they want to do what mama and papa are doing.

—Quote

745.   There is no surer delinquency in a child than truancy from school.

746.   If Billy the Kid was under 21, as they say, how come he was allowed in saloons?

747.   One father at a PTA meeting said to another that when he was a boy he was whipped so much he thought he was a dog team.

748.   Juvenile delinquency is nothing more that the fruit which has grown from the seeds of parent delinquency, religious delinquency, educational delinquency, judiciary delinquency and municipal delinquency.

—Dr. Vincent Mazzola

K

Kindergarten (See Children, Schools, Students, Teachers)

749.   There was a sudden commotion in the kindergarten class, and the teacher looked up to see one of the youngsters fighting with a little girl.

"Henry," said the teacher, "why are you hitting Linda?"

"We were playing Adam and Eve," he replied tearfully, "but she ate all the apple before she tempted me!"

Kindergarten (See Children, Schools, Students, Teachers)

750.   On the opening day of school:

Eighty-four percent of the new kindergartners vowed, "I'm not going to school today, tomorrow or ever!"

Eighteen million mothers watched their solemn youngsters leave home. Gratefully, they sighed, "God bless school."

Two million eight hundred thousand teachers commented, "There must be an easier way to make a living."

751.   Mrs. Ruth Watt told her kindergarten class in the Indian Hills School in River Hills, "Next week, each of you can bring a pet to school to show each other."

Four year old Kathie Zieve of Bayside raised her hand to ask a question.

"I don't have a pet," she said. "Can I bring my mommy?"

752.   "How's Mike doing in kindergarten?"

"Not very good. He flunked clay."

753.   A kindergarten teacher putting her charges through a psychological test set them to work carving soap. "Panda, dog, man, table, tree, gun, car," she wrote as the tots told her what they were making.

Then she came to a boy whose work appeared to defy description. "What's this?" she asked. "Soap flakes," he said.

754.   Kindergarten teachers learn to be just a bit cautious about accepting stories brought to school by their pupils.

One little girl announced that her father had died the night before. The entire class saddened, and took up a little collection to send flowers.

The teacher wondered why the child missed no school during the period of bereavement. She didn't really become suspicious, however, until the little girl announced several days later that her mother was remarrying "a man she met at the funeral home."

755.   The boy who got a wrist watch when he graduated from high school now has a son who wears one to kindergarten.

756.   Overheard in local kindergarten:

"Johnny, it's just a scratch, please don't cry."

"I'm not gonna cry—I'm gonna sue!"

757.   Is the head of the house at home?" a salesman asked.
"No," replied the mother. "He's in kindergarten right now."

758.   With tears in his eyes, the little boy told his kindergarten teacher that only one pair of galoshes was left in the cloakroom and they weren't his.

The teacher searched under chairs and in corners, but could find no other galoshes. Exhausted, she asked the boy, "How can you be sure that these galoshes aren't yours?"

The boy replied: "Mine had snow on them."

–Brian Morin
Boy's Life

759.   Kindergarten Teacher: "What is it that zebras have that no other animals have?"

Kindergartner: "Little zebras."

760.   Father: "And what did you learn in kindergarten today?"
Son: "I learned to say 'Yes, sir' and 'No, sir' and 'Yes, ma'am' and 'No, ma'am.' "
Father: "You did?"
Son: "Yep."

761.   Teacher: "You said that your father fell off a ladder and hurt himself? What did he say?"
Little Boy: "Shall I leave out the bad words?"
Teacher: "Of course, Johnny."
Little Boy: "Nothing!"

Kindness (See Happiness)

762.   Kindness is one thing you can't give away—it always comes back.

763.   The kindest are those who forgive and forget.

764.   Teacher, answering door: "Have you been offered any work?"

Knowlege (See Education, Genius, School, Teachers)

Reliefer: "Only once. Aside from that I've met with nothing but kindness."

765.   The teacher of a class of young boys asked them to tell the meaning of loving kindness.

One pupil replied: "If I was hungry and someone gave me a piece of bread and butter, that would be kindness. But if they put lots of jam on it, that would be loving kindness."

> —Mrs. Berthene Runninger
> *Together*

Knowledge (See Education, Genius, School, Teachers)

766.   Knowledge and timber shouldn't be much used till they are seasoned.

> —Oliver Wendell Holmes

767.   Knowledge, like any other tool, is a good investment when put to constructive use.

768.   The only commodity on earth that does not deteriorate with use is knowledge.

> *—Sunshine*

L

Language (See English, Grammar, Spelling, Words)

769.   A firefly is not a fly and glow worm is not a worm. Actually, both are beetles.
The wood called Douglas fir is from the pine tree.
Every dressed chicken is practically nude.
Dry cleaning is made possible with a liquid.
Squirrel fur is used in the manufacture of Camel's hair brushes.
The Caraway seed is not seed. It is a fruit that has dried.
French telephones were originally American.

770. Evidently, the American language (American, not English) is changing. We just ran across a short glossary of pioneer American slang, and it is colorful stuff. For example, if a frontiersman had wanted to say that Smith, a good man, had lost a political race to his no-good opponent, he might have said:

"Smitty's a real teetotacious ripstaver, he is, but he got plumb obfisticated and ramsquaddled by that tarnacious ring-tailed roarer!"

In modern American slang, it might sound more like this:

"Smith's top-flight. But charisma-wise, he's nowhere, and so the other party just flat destructed him."

771. A teacher left Ireland and came to live in America. After a year he sent for his wife and children. "Goodness," she exclaimed on her first day, "But don't they talk funny in America."

" "You think they talk funny now!" exclaimed her husband. "Why, you should have heard them when I first got here!"

Law

772. The law professor was lecturing on classroom procedure. "When you are fighting a case and have the facts on your side, hammer the facts. If you have the law on your side, hammer the law."

"But if you don't have the facts or law," asked a student "what do you do?"

"In that case," the professor replied "hammer on the table."

773. Law is the merriest game of chance in the world. Nobody has any idea what a law really is, or how the judge will apply it, or finally, what the jury will do.

—Miami Herald

774. Clothes don't make the man, but a good suit makes a lawyer.

—Today's Chuckle

775. A recent graduate from law school was so devoted to his profession that he christened his daughter, "Sue."

776. "How is it you extracted a watch from that man's pocket without his knowing it?" asked the judge.

"My fee is $5 for the full course of ten lessons, your honor."

777. The law professor was describing a case to his class in which a new lawyer had been retained by a farmer to prosecute a railroad for killing twenty-four of his hogs. It was his first case and the young lawyer wanted to make every point of his argument impressive and to impress the jury with the magnitude of the damage.

"Twenty-four hogs, gentlemen!" he cried. "Think of it! Twenty-four! Twice the number of you in the jury box!"

778. A jury consists of twelve persons chosen to decide who has the better lawyer.

—Robert Frost

779. Some day, the "law and order" citizens may wake up and demand equal riots.

780. In commenting on the consequences of perjury to his student law class, the professor cited the instance of the witness who kept lying in the courtroom.

"Do you realize what the penalty will be if you keep lying like this?" said the judge.

"I presume I'll go to Hell," said the witness.

"Yes, but what else?" asked the judge.

The witness thought for a minute and then answered, "Well, isn't that enough?"

781. Student Lawyer: "And I quote the words of the immortal Daniel Webster, the compiler of this dictionary—"

Professor: "That wasn't Daniel Webster, that was Noah!"

Student Lawyer: "Noah, nothing. Noah built the ark."

782. Judge: a law student who marks his own examination papers.

—H.L. Mencken

783.   There is but one law for all: namely the law which governs all law—the law of our Creator, the law of humanity, justice, equality and the law of nature and of nations.

—Edmund Burke

784.   A bad agreement is better than a good law suit.

785.   What we need is a child labor law to keep parents of college students from working themselves to death.

786.   Law gives pedestrians the right of way, but makes no provision for the consequences.

787.   Man is a creative creature. He has made millions of laws but hasn't improved on the Ten Commandments.

788.   Father: "Then your law professor I understand is elderly?"
Student: "Elderly? Why, he's so old he gets winded playing chess."

Leadership (See Ambition, Success)

789.   "The trouble with being a leader these days is that you can't be sure whether people are following you or chasing you."

790.   Leadership in teaching is the art of getting somebody else to learn something you want him to learn because he wants to learn it.

791.   The greatest strides of human progress have come from uncommon men and women, like George Washington, Abraham Lincoln and Thomas Edison.
When we get sick, we want an uncommon doctor. When we go to war, we yearn for an uncommon general or admiral. When we choose the president of a university, we want an uncommon educator.
The imperative need of this Nation at all times is the leadership of the uncommon men and women. We need men and women who cannot be

133

intimidated, who are not concerned with applause meters, who will not sell tomorrow for cheers today.

−Herbert Hoover

Library (See Books, Words)

792.   The young boy appeared at the librarian's desk with a book he wanted to take out. The title was: "What Every Young Mother Should Know."

The librarian raised her eyebrows and asked the youngster why he would want to read such a book.

"Well," he replied, "I'm collecting moths."

793.   Two small boys were in a school library, chattering away at the top of their voices. The librarian hurried over. "Ssh!" she said, "The people in this room can't read."

One of the boys looked at her with sympathy: "Dropouts, huh?"

794.   Remember when the librarian kept risque novels in the bottom drawer of her desk?

−Lois Pflughoeft, in the
Algoma Record-Herald

Liberation Movement (See Family Life, Parenthood)

795.   The year's biggest breakthrough in women's liberation takes place when schools open in the fall.

Life (See Age, Happiness, Middle Age, Time, Youth)

796.   "Life demands from you only the strength you possess," said Dag Hamarskjold. "Only one feat is possible−not to have run away."

797.   A supervisor says, "I'm just one of those inbetween citizens who is at the wrong age and position in life: Too young for Social Security and Medicare, too prosperous for welfare, too urban for crop subsidies, and too American to receive foreign aid."

798.   A horse can't pull while kicking.
This fact I merely mention.
And he can't kick while pulling.
Which is my chief contention.
Let's imitate the good old horse
And lead a life that's fitting;
Just pull an honest load, and then . . .
There'll be no time for kicking.

799.   All people come into the world not knowing anything and many will go out the same way.

800.   I believe first and foremost that life is not merely worth living but intensely precious, and that the supreme object in life is to live.

—Julian S. Huxley

801.   Today is the first day of the rest of your life. Make it count.

802.   Living dangerously has been defined as having the living room sofa reupholstered while the children are still under 12.

—Margaret Lee, in the *Deerfield Independent*

803.   Short as life is, some find it long enough to outlive their characters, their constitutions and their estates.

—Caleb Colton

804.   The trouble with living it up is—you may have to live it down later.

—Bob Wright, in the *Marguette County Tribune*, Montello

805.   One's age should be tranquil as childhood should be playful. Hard work at either extremity of life seems out of place.

—Matthew Arnold

806. George Washington Carver, the Negro Botanist, chemist and educator (1864-1943) whose research developed profitable uses of such humble crops as the peanut and the soybean, often summarized his life philosophy with this story:

"When I was young, I said to God, 'God, tell me the mystery of the universe.'

"But God answered, 'That knowledge is reserved for Me alone.'

"So I said, 'God, tell me the mystery of the peanut.'

"Then God said, 'Well, George, that's more nearly your size,' And He told me."

That, for some reason, seems to us to be one of the greatest little stories ever told. It's a peanut-sized story, but it has universe-sized meanings in it. Like the saying about the great oak growing from the tiny acorn, it seems to be an illustration of the way greatness is related to humility.

And it seems to tell us, too, how we find in our acceptance of small wonders in the seed of great faith.

George Washington Carver evidently believed there was an affinity between himself and the lowly peanut. From this belief there grew an almost immeasurable usefulness which filled his life.

And if the usefulness of life is not a great universal answer, we don't know what is.

—Nuggets

807. Two can live as cheaply as one, but it takes both to earn enough to do it.

808. The biggest problem in life is how to stay in the groove without making it into a rut. This timely bit of advice was handed to us on the street and we can't remember by whom.

809. One of the oddest things about modern life is the number of people who are spending money they haven't got for things they don't want, to impress people they can't stand the sight of.

—Catholic Digest

810. It is an irony of life that we get bent from hard work and broke without it.

Literature (See English, Language, Writing)

811. At least one local high school freshman has been more influenced by movie publicity than he has by Shakespeare's play, "Romeo and Juliet," which he and his classmates are reading.

In taking class notes, he called one scene the bed scene, to the astonishment of his teacher and probably Will Shakespeare if he was watching.

—Sam, in the *Reedsburg Times-Press*

812. A teacher in an English literature class in Wausau East High School, concluding a study of "Ode to the West Wind," asked her class what Shelley meant by the line: "If winter comes, can spring be far behind?"

A voice from the rear of the room:

"It means that Shelley never spent a winter in Wisconsin! He wouldn't have to ask!"

—*Milwaukee Journal*

813. "Papa, what kind of a robber is a page?"

"A what?"

"It says here that two pages held up the bride's train."

814. It was the beginning of a new term at State University and the professor was asking the members of his class various questions to determine the knowledge of his students.

"Are you acquainted with Shakespeare?" he asked one student.

"Not personally," the student replied "but he's a great friend of my brother."

"Your brother!" exclaimed the professor. "Why Shakespeare has been dead for 300 years," he said angrily.

"He has?" exclaimed the student. "Say, won't my brother be surprised to hear that!"

Logic (See Education)

815. Illogical logic: The bigger a man's head grows, the easier it is to fill his shoes.

Loneliness

816. "Logic" is an organized procedure for going wrong with confidence and certainty.

—Earl Wilson

817. Logic is the art of teaching us of some truth.

—Bruyere

818. Abraham Lincoln was noted for winning many an argument from sheer force of logic. The story is told of one occasion when he used logic to make an opponent see the error of his reasoning.

"How many legs has a cow?" asked Lincoln

"Four, of course," came the reply.

"That's right," said Lincoln. "Now suppose we call the cow's tail a leg, how many legs would the cow have?"

"Why, five," was the answer.

"Not true," said Lincoln. "Simply calling a cow's tail a leg doesn't make it a leg."

Loneliness

819. Many people are lonely because they build walls instead of bridges.

Love (See Family Life, Friendship, Happiness)

820. Young Steve's first four months at kindergarten apparently widened his horizons considerably, so his mother thought it would be interesting to inquire about his current loyalties.

"Honey," she said, "whom do you love best?"

Soberly he considered the question and then replied, "Well, I love you best. And then comes Daddy. And teacher is last. But in between come a lot of dogs."

821. Love is an emptiness that students feel first in the pit of their stomachs, then in their heads, and finally in their wallets.

822. Love is what makes a teacher spend $35 in veterinary fees on a $5 dog.

—*Milwaukee Journal*

823.   When a man falls in love with himself, it's usually the beginning of a life-long romance.

Loyalty (See America, School, Tradition)

824.   Loyalty is the inheritance tax we should be willing to pay on our American Heritage.

Lunch (See Home Economics)

825.   At the beginning of the year, before the lunch program started, I took my first-graders down to the lunch room to explain procedures. I assigned tables, explained how to carry the trays and how to behave. As we returned to our classroom, I overheard one little boy remark, "What a dumb teacher. She forgot to let us eat!"

—Mildred C. Higgins
Georgetown, S.C.

826.   Because a friend of mine has always insisted that his children eat all the food on their plates, his youngsters were undismayed when the school lunchroom adopted a policy forbidding second helpings and dessert to anyone who hadn't cleaned up his plate.

Sometime later, when the youngest son, Scott, asked for a bicycle for his birthday, his father said that a bike cost more than he expected to spend. Scott offered to pay half. "I've got $33," he said, and produced a cache of coins filling a large cigar box. Fearing thievery at the least or extortion at the worst, my friend demanded to know how his son had acquired such a hoard.

"I earned it at school," Scott replied simply. "You see, the kids pay me to eat the vegetables they don't like. I charge a nickel for spinach, a dime for broccoli or cauliflower, and 15 cents for sauerkraut."

—John J. Ward, *Readers' Digest*

M

Mankind (See Parenthood, Life, Men & Women, Family)

827.   The man who sits all day on a riverbank and watches his fishing pole is considered a patient man. The man who sits on his front porch all day and contemplates the passing world is a lazy bum.

828. If a man runs after money, he's money mad; if he keeps it, he's a capitalist; if he spends it, he's a playboy; if he doesn't get it, he's a ne'er-do-well; if he doesn't try to get it, he lacks ambition; if he gets it without working for it, he's a parasite; and if he accumulates it after a lifetime of hard work, people call him a fool who never got anything out of life.

—Vic Oliver

829. Men may be smarter than women, but you never see a woman marry a dumb man just because he happens to have a good figure.

—Today's Chuckle

830. Man hasn't really changed much through the ages. He has, of course, progressed to the point where he walks upright—but his eyes still swing from limb to limb.

—Chatham Blanketeer, Today's Chuckle

831. Is it a man's world? Maybe. But compare these frequently heard descriptions of male and female.

If a woman is short, she's "petite." If a man is short, he's a "runt."

Lacking bravery, a woman is "timid"—a man is a "coward."

A woman who is inept at earning a living is the "domestic type." But a man who is inept at earning a living is a "ne'er-do-well."

An unworldly girl is "innocent." An unworldly man "isn't dry behind the ears."

The woman with a job in a masculine field, such as engineering, is a "pioneer." A male fashion designer is a "sissy."

A girl stays single because she "prefers a career." A man stays single because he is "egotistical" and "selfish."

A woman who jilts a man is merely exercising a "feminine prerogative." A man who jilts a woman is "cruel" and "heartless."

When a couple gets married, a girl is "set for life." The man is "hooked."

—Dan Bennett, *Family Weekly*

832. There are three classes of men, the ambitious, the intelligent and the majority.

—The Rice Lake Chronotype

Manners (See Tact)

833.   Politeness and good breeding are absolutely necessary to adorn any or all other good qualities or talents. Without them ... the scholar is a pedant, the philosopher a cynic, the soldier a brute and every man disagreeable.

—Lord Chesterfield

834.   Manners are the happy ways of doing things.
—Ralph Waldo Emerson

835.   Etiquette means behaving yourself a little better than is absolutely essential.

—Will Cuppy

836.   Too much of the world is run on the theory that you don't need road manners if you are a five ton truck.

—*El Paso Herald*

837.   Good manners is made up of petty sacrifices.

—Emerson

838.   Lack of students' manners can be attributed to the fact that the old woodshed has been replaced by the garage.

Mathematics (See Accounting, Computer, Education, Students)

839.   Toward the end of the school year, the sixth-grade teachers decide which of their students should be accelerated in certain subjects in the seventh grade. When a child is chosen, his parents are notified.

When one boy was accelerated in science and math, his mother wrote to the teacher: "I think this is quite an honor for someone who just tried to make two quarts of lemonade in a one-quart pitcher!"

—*Readers' Digest*

Mathematics (See Accounting, Computer, Education, Students)

840.   Teacher: "If your mother gave you a large apple and a small one and told you to divide with your brother, which would you give him?"

Johnnie: "Do you mean my little brother or my big brother?"

841.   Marilyn: Daddy, how do you find the least common denominator?

Dad: Great Scott! They haven't found that yet? They were looking for it when I was in school.

842.   If you think marriage is a 50-50 proposition, you've flunked your course in fractions.

843.   While experimenting, a Greek mathematician found one number which behaves very strangely when it is multiplied. It is the six-figure number 142,857. When it is multiplied by 2, the result is 285,714—the same figures, differently arranged! The same phenomenon is repeated when it is multiplied by 3. The result is 428,571. Multiply it by 4, we find 571,428 and multiplying it by 5 we have 714,285. When it is multiplied by 6 the group of figures in the basic number merely changes, becoming 857,142. Continue this multiplication and at 7 times, the number suddenly equals 999,999.

844.   "Now remember," said the instructor, "figures never lie. Take, for example, the building of a house. If 12 men could build a house in one day, one man could build that same house in 12 days. Do you understand? James you give me another example."

"Sure," answered James with a smile. "You mean that if one boat could cross the ocean in six days, six boats could cross the ocean in one day."

845.   "Why did you drop your math course?"

"The math professor goes so deep that every time I tried to follow him I got the bends."

—John Gillespie

846.   A teacher is trying to teach a young student how to add and subtract simple items in his head, but with little success. She tries a new approach.

Teacher: "Look Mike, make believe you can see a blackboard in your mind. Can you see it?"

Mike: "Yes."

Teacher: "Good, now write down 2 plus 2." Facial contortions of agony appear on Mike's face.

Teacher: "What's wrong?"

Mike: "I can't find the chalk."

847.   The seven-year-old came home from school looking disgusted and her mother asked her what the difficulty was.

"I'm having trouble in school with the eagles," replied the youngster.

"Eagles . . . in school?" asked the baffled mother.

"You know," said the girl. "Two plus two eagles four. Three plus three eagles six . . . "

848.   "No wonder, Jeanne gets straight A's in French," said one teenager to another. "Her parents are Parisians and they speak French at home."

"Then I ought to get A in geometry," complained the other. "My parents are squares and they talk in circles."

849.   A grandmother was asked one day by her granddaughter, Vicky, if she were going to have a birthday soon.

"In a couple of weeks," the grandmother said.

"Then, grandma, you'll be 40."

"No, Vicky. I'll be 39."

"But you were 39 last birthday," Vicky protested.

"Yes, I was 39 last year and the year before and the year before that and I'm going to keep on being 39."

Vicky thought that over for a while.

"Grandma," she finally asked, "is that old math or the new math?"

850.   One of the arithmetic problems dealt with the number of feet of material needed for a certain project. The book went on to ask, "The two numerals in the problem mean feet, so what will the answer mean?"

"Toes," responded one little girl.

—Eleanor Wright, Kansas City

851.   Teacher: "If you had seven pieces of candy and I asked for four, how many would you have left?"

Student: "Seven."

852.   Teacher: "If you had three apples and someone gave you five more, what would you have?"

Mike: "A belly ache!"

853.   Professor: "It gives me great pleasure to give you eighty-one in mathematics."

Student: "Why don't you make it one hundred and *really* enjoy yourself."

854.   There is no royal road to geometry.

—Euclid

855.   Women have a passion for arithmetic. They divide their ages by two, double the price of their clothes, triple their husbands' salaries, and add five years to the ages of their best friends.

856.   The teacher was trying to get over the intricacies of subtraction. "You have ten fingers," she said. "Suppose you had three less, then what would you have?"

"No music lessons," Tommy replied promptly.

857.   Teacher: "What is a half?"

Student: "Half is when you cut something into two pieces and don't care which one the other fellow takes."

858.   In a follow-up program evaluation, researchers tracked down the first college graduate who was educated in New Math all the way. It was a lot of fun at the time, he recalled, but in the two years he's been out of school, he was yet to meet a cashier or a bill collector who wasn't still operating on Base 10.

—*National Observer*

859.   You can't teach an old dad new math.

—Joann Thomas

860.   Math teacher: "Now, if I lay three eggs here and five eggs over there, how many eggs will I have laid?"

Student: "Well, to tell you the truth, sir, I don't believe you can do it."

Medicine (See Mental Health, Psychiatry, Weight and Diet)

861. A physician is a man who always treats at the other fellow's expense.

862. Anyone who has paid an obstetrician's fee knows that Americans aren't born free.

863. Mrs. Brown was complaining to her doctor that his bill was unreasonably high. "Don't forget," he reminded her, "that I made eleven visits to your home while your son had the measles."

"And don't you forget," she countered, "that he infected the whole school."

864. A student asked his professor what he thought a certain operation would be worth.

"About a hundred dollars."

"Would it be a dangerous operation?" the student asked.

"Oh, no," replied the professor. "You can't buy a dangerous operation for a hundred dollars."

865. A young graduate doctor received a phone call from one of his colleagues inviting him to play poker.

"Going out, dear?" asked his wife.

"I'm afraid so," he replied gravely. "It's a very important case. Four doctors are there already."

866. We've finally figured out what doctors scribble on those prescriptions to druggists: "I've got my $10—now he's all yours."

Memory (See Ability, Absent Minded, Professors)

867. "Why is that string tied around your finger, Bobby?" asked his teacher.

"My mom put it there to remind me to mail her letter on my way to school today."

"Did you mail it?"

"Sure."

"Then why don't you take the string off?"

" 'Cause I need it to remind me to tell her that she forgot to put a stamp on the letter."

868. Memory, retentiveness and the ability to recall represent a talent or a sense that people seem to have in varying degrees. It is a valuable asset to those in certain business or social positions ... and sometimes we envy those people who have an uncanny ability to remember names, places, events.

869. Man and woman at Marriage Counselor's Office. He says, "Whatsername here says I'm forgetful."

870. Some people have such poor memories that they can't remember what comes after Walla.

–Pic Larmour submitted by Gene
Freehan

871. Some years ago, a series of ads appeared regularly in school papers and magazines extolling the virtues of a famous memory course. They depicted two men meeting on the street and one of them was saying: "I remember you—you're Addison Sims of Seattle." I can recall all that vividly ... but I can't remember the name of the memory course.

872. A professor went to his doctor and complained about the fact that he was losing his memory. He said: "Doc, I just can't seem to remember anything from one moment to the next." The doctor said: "How long has this been going on?" and the professor said: "How long has what been going on?"

873. An instructor who can't remember his postal Zip Code Number, will very likely forget his wife's birthday.

874. Memory is like an eraser. It often rubs out past mistakes.

875.   A poor memory is about the most effective defense against spreading a rumor.

876.   If you want to remember things, tie a string around your finger. To forget, tie a rope around your neck.

877.   "My wife has the worst memory I ever heard of," remarked the teacher to a colleague.
"You mean she forgets everything?" he asked.
"No, she remembers everything."

878.   A man with a clear conscience may be one with just a poor memory.

879.   Everyone complains of his memory; nobody of his judgment.

—La Rochefoucauld

880.   Memory seldom fails when its office is to show us the tombs of our buried hopes.

—Lady Blessington

881.   Memory is the receptacle and sheath of all knowledge.
—Cicero

Men and Women (See Parenthood)

882.   We were talking about the equality of the sexes the other day, and one of the instructors on our teaching staff said that a woman can never be a man's equal until she can sport a large bald spot on the top of her head and still think she's handsome.

883.   Pablo Picasso, the famous painter and sculptor, evidently has a much more orderly mind than his pictures and statues would indicate. It is said that a girl reporter who was interviewing him once asked why mature men generally look younger than mature women. Picasso thought for a moment, then suggested: "It is because a woman of forty is usually fifty."

—*Nuggets*

884.   It's a man's world, and for men it's rosy.
For men INVESTIGATE; women are NOSY.
Men STAND FIRM; women are MULISH.
The male's INDISCREET; the female's FOOLISH.
The man TAKES CREDIT; the woman is BRAGGING.
A man is CRITICAL; the woman is NAGGING.
Men MAKE CONCESSIONS; women SURRENDER.
But, nevertheless, the feminine gender
Has one advantage it well deserves:
Men have TEMPERS; women have NERVES!

—Author Unknown

885.   Many of the differences between men and women are almost intangible. Researches report these oddities in *Sales Management Magazine:* Men walk from the knee; women, from the hip. Men strike matches toward themselves; women, away. Men dress to look like other men; women, to look unique in current fashion. Men look at their fingernails by cupping their palms and bending their fingers toward themselves; women extend their fingers outward. Men nag their wives for what they do; wives nag their husbands for what they don't do.

Mental Health (See Medicine, Psychiatrist)

886.   A new school doctor thought the student looked normal and asked him why he was going to a psychiatrist. "It's because I prefer cotton socks to woolen ones," said the patient.

"Ridiculous! that's no reason for sending you here," said the doctor. "I prefer cotton socks, too."

The patient beamed. "I'm glad to hear that, doc! Tell me, how do you like them? With oil and vinegar or just a squeeze of lemon?"

Middle Age (See Age, Youth)

887.   Middle age is the time when your memory is shorter, your experience longer, your stamina lower and your forehead higher.

888.   Middle age is that time in life when your narrow waist and broad mind start to change places.

889.   Middle age is the time in life when you're still young, but only once in a while.

890.　　　Middle age is the time of life when we exchange ambitions for symptoms.

891.　　　Middle age is when you are old enough to know better, but young enough to keep on doing it.

892.　　　Middle age is when you are grounded for several days after flying high the night before.

Military (See History)

893.　　　While discussing Veteran's Day in a third-grade class, the teacher asked her pupils if they knew the meaning of the word "veteran."

One youngster volunteered. "A veteran is a person who eats only vegetables," he said.

Immediately, another youngster corrected him. "That's not right. A veteran is an animal doctor."

894.　　　A fellow student who had just returned from the war in Vietnam was asked where he was from.

"Well," he said "I was born in Wisconsin but I grew up in Vietnam."

895.　　　A history teacher was bearing down on disarmament and peace.

"How many in the class dislike war?"

She singled out a boy and said; "All right, John, you tell us why you don't like war?"

"Because wars make history," he replied seriously.

896.　　　"The only way I'd like to go back into service," said one student to another, "would be as a commander of an LMD."

"What's an LMD?" asked his friend.

"Why that's a Long Mahogany Desk."

Miniskirts (See Teenagers)

897.　　　The miniskirt fad allowed some mothers to wear their young daughter's clothes. They're sort of hand-me-ups.

898.   Miniskirts rank in advancement equal with the steamboat. As Robert Fulton put it, "We no longer have to wait for the wind to blow."

899.   The first miniskirts were "Eve's leaves."

900.   We have to credit the miniskirt to making men more polite. You never saw a man get on a bus ahead of one.

901.   In a poll, 40% of the men questioned were opposed to women wearing miniskirts. The other 60% were so busy watching the miniskirts that they didn't hear the question.

902.   Fashion turned away from the miniskirt trend. Designers were slowly working themselves out of a job.

903.   When the miniskirt trend developed, mothers approved wholeheartedly of it. They finally found a fashion where their daughters left mother's clothes alone.

904.   The miniskirt trend also developed a new type of glasses by opticians. They were called "thigh-focals."

905.   The boy who tried to hide behind his mother's miniskirt had to stand on a high chair.

Misfortune (See Mistakes, Problems)

906.   A teacher asked her 7th graders for a definition of misery. Here are the answers: Misery is an eight-year-old brother. Misery is having to change the goldfish water. Misery is taking French lessons. Misery is doing the wrong page of mathematics. Misery is dressing up for church and then finding out it's only Saturday. Misery is going into the lunchroom feeling very hungry, only to find out they're having beets.

907.   An instructor was moving along a dimly-lighted street when a stranger slipped from the shadows and stopped him. "What do you want?" asked the man nervously.

"Would you be so kind," said the stranger plaintively, "as to help a poor unfortunate fellow who is hungry and out of work? All I have in the world is this gun."

Mistakes (See Misfortune)

908. "There are about three things a fellow can do when he makes a mistake," said the teacher to a class of boys. "He can resolve that he will never make another, which is fine but impractical. He may let that mistake make a coward of him, which is foolish; or he can make up his mind that he'll let it be his teacher and so profit by the experience that if the situation comes his way again, he'll know just how to meet it."

909. "The trouble with some students," said the instructor to his class, "is that they won't admit their faults. "Why, I'd be the first one to admit my faults," he continued, "if I had any."

Moonlighting

910. Moonlighter: A teacher who holds both day and night jobs so he can drive from one to the other in a better car.

911. Moonlighting might be described as burning the candle at both ends in order to make ends meet.

912. There's the story of the teacher who moonlighted as a used car salesman and then went into the television selling business. Now his sales pitch goes like this:
"This used TV set has hardly been used. It belonged to an old lady with weak eyes."

Motherhood (See Children, Parenthood)

913. A woman teacher traveling alone on an airplane leaned over and said to a woman who was traveling with her two small children: "I'd give ten years of my life to have a couple of fine, active youngsters like those."
"That," declared the mother, "Is just about what they cost."

Movies (See Television, Theater)

914. The projectionist at one of our local drive-in movies didn't show up until 10 P.M. the other night and nobody missed him.

Music (See Music Instruction, Theater)

915. A friend of ours reports an odd experience at the local campus drive-in movie. He said that he watched a love scene for 25 minutes before he realized he was facing in the wrong direction.

916. A mother and her teen-age daughter were watching a 1930 film on TV. As it ended with the usual romantic clinch and fadeout of that era, the teenager observed. "Gosh, Mom, your movies end where ours begin."

917. Some of the movie epics are really long. We can remember when it took a whole lot longer to read the book than to see the show.

918. Remember when a rating X was only on your long division.

919. A cameraman working for the University film department met an old farmer in town and said:
"I've been taking some movies of life on your farm."
"Did you catch any of my men in motion?" asked the farmer.
"Sure I did."
The farmer shook his head, and then commented. "Science is a wonderful thing."

Music (See Music Instruction, Theater)

920. "Is that a popular song he's singing?" asked a student at a concert.
"It was before he sang it," replied his friend.

921. The piano teacher was expected any minute and Tommy was preparing to take his lesson.
"Did you wash your hands?" inquired his mother.
"Yes."
"And your face?"
"Yes, mother."
"And did you wash behind your ears?"
"On her side I did, mother."

922. A grandmother, who had tried to instill in her children and grandchildren a love of music, said her heart leaped the other day when she heard her nine-year-old grandson whistling Mendelssohn's Spring Song as he half-heartedly went about doing his homework.

"Where did you learn that music?" she asked the lad.

"Oh, that?" he said. "That's what they play on television when someone gets bopped on the head."

923. A young student was late for the symphony concert. "What are they playing now?" she breathlessly asked the usher.

"The Ninth Symphony," he replied.

"Goodness!" she exclaimed, "am I as late as that?"

924. Sometimes the best thing about a popular song is that it isn't popular too long.

925. Small boy at piano to his mother:

"Gee, Mommy, I wish you hadn't been deprived of so many things as a child."

926. Little girl witnessing her first Benediction Service. She watched, fascinated, as the altar boy lit all the candles. Then she turned to her mother and asked, "Mommie, is Liberace coming?"

927. The real music lover is the young student's wife who applauds when her husband comes home singing at 3 o'clock in the morning.

928. Student (at school concert): "What's that book the conductor keeps looking at?"

Escort: "That's the score of the overture."

She: "Oh, really, who's winning?"

929. "You say your son plays the piano like a concert pianist?" the instructor asked his friend.

"Yes, he uses both hands."

Music Instruction (See Music, Theater)

930.   "Music is a thing of the soul, an instrument of God," wrote Eugene P. Bertin in the Pennsylvania School Journal. "It lightens labor and speeds play, it soothes the sad, refreshes the weary, breaks human barriers, stirs patriotic impulses and dignifies the activities of mankind. It is the ultimate form of culture."

931.   Frank Dickson in Quote tells this one: The lengthy recital had ended, ice cream and cake had been served and the teacher was bidding the students goodbye. One of the little performers had brought her small brother with her. As he was about to leave, the teacher beaming asked, "Well, Bobby, did you enjoy the recital?"
"Yes," Bobby answered, "all but the music."

932.   Modern music is the kind that is played so fast you can't tell what classical composer it was stolen from.

933.   The first thing a child learns when he gets a drum is that he's never going to get another one.

Music Instruction (See Music, Theater)

934.   "I'm warning you," said the exasperated piano teacher to her pupil, "if you don't behave yourself, I'll tell your parents you have talent."

935.   The host's small daughter was asked by a guest, "Do you play on the piano, dear?"
The little girl replied: "Not when Mom's around. She'd be afraid I'd fall off."

—Dorothea Kent

N

Nature Study (See Animals, Biology, Zoology)

936.   A school teacher was giving her small pupils a lesson on birds, and after telling them about the hatching of the eggs, the care of the mother bird and the first lessons in flying she said: "Now, children, I am the mother bird and you are the little birds nestled in your cozy nest. I want you all to spread your wings and fly away."

Each child, waving arms to the music she beat, skipped to the dressing room with the exception of one little fellow, who remained in his seat.

Turning to him, she said: "Donald, why didn't you fly away with all the other little birds?"

"Cause," came the reply. "I was a rotten egg."

937.   Teacher: "Ted, you tell the class what an oyster is?"
Ted: "It's a fish built like a nut."

938.   Teacher: "What is a bee?"
Student: "A fly insect with a stinger .3215 inches long. The other ten inches is your imagination."

939.   Teacher: "And to what family does the whale belong?"
Student: "I don't know, ma'am. No one in my neighborhood has one."

940.   In a nature study class in elementary school, a laboratory rabbit outlived its usefulness, and the teacher decided to get rid of it by holding a drawing, with the child who pulled the lucky number from a hat getting the rabbit. Each child was asked to bring a note from home saying he could bring the rabbit home if he won it.

The next afternoon, one little boy rushed home carrying the rabbit in its chicken-wire cage. His parents' hearts sank, but they tried to act glad. "Well," they said. "So you drew the lucky number, out of all those pupils!"

"Uh, no," said the boy, "they didn't draw a number out of the hat after all. But I was the only one with a note."

–Nuggets

O

Opinion (See Egotism, Envy)

941.   Yawning in class may be bad manners, but at least it is an honest opinion.

155

Opportunity (See Ambition, Determination, Education, Traits)

942. It is much better to tell people how to get on than to tell them where to get off.

943. One of the hardest secrets for a PhD to keep is his opinion of himself.

944. Some people who ask for your candid opinion, really want it candied.

—Parsons, *Kan. SUN*

945. The one weakness of some public opinion is that people express it only in private.

946. Opinion is something that is often handed down from generation to generation . . . and never changed.

Opportunity (See Ambition, Determination, Education, Traits)

947. It's funny how much bigger opportunities look going than coming.

948. Opportunities are never lost. The other teacher takes those you've missed.

949. There's plenty of opportunity in a land where even a horse can make a million dollars.

950. The trouble with too many students these days is that they want to get to the promised land without going through the wilderness.

951. Many students miss opportunity because it usually comes disguised as hard work.

952. There's only one endeavor in which you can start at the top, and that's digging a hole.

—*L & N Magazine*

953. The bottom rung of a ladder *should* be the strongest. It supports the most people.

954. Confucius say: No man who catch large fish go home through alley.

—C.A. Vig in the *Bee Phillips*

955. People may not hear opportunity knock if they are off looking for four-leaf clovers.

956. Any instructor who does not know how to make the most of his luck has no right to complain if it passes him by.

957. If your ship won't come in, chances are you just haven't dug the harbor deep enough.

958. The only reason there is plenty of room at the top is that those coming up keep pushing the top ones off.

959. If opportunity knocked on the heads of some students instead of their doors, there might be better results.

960. Temptation doesn't have to break down the door; opportunity won't.

Outer Space (See Exploration, Science)

961. The kindergarten children were working diligently to draw a picture of Col. Glenn's orbits around the earth.

The first girl finished her picture and brought it to the teacher.

"Lovely, lovely," said the teacher, "but who is this lady down in the corner?"

"Oh, I thought you'd know," said the little girl. "That's Kate Canavarel."

962. "Do you think there is intelligent life in outer space," asked the professor.

"Sure do," replied one of his students. "You don't see anyone else wasting $30 billion to find out about us."

963.   The astronaut was poised in his space craft, ready to be launched.

"How do you feel," asked one of the reporters.

"How would you feel," the astronaut replied "if you were sitting on top of 150,000 parts—each supplied by the lowest bidder?"

—N.D. *Official Bulletin*

964.   A Russian, an American and a French teacher were indulging in a bit of boasting at an educational conference. "By 1980" asserted the American teacher, "we'll have colonies on the moon, with people popping up there from New York for the week-end."

"Bah," scoffed the Russian. "By that time Russia will have shown up America by settling on Mars. The moon will just be a way station for us."

The French teacher, not to be outdone, said: "By that time we will put an astronaut on the sun."

"How can you say such a foolish thing," the other two said. "Don't you realize that a man on the sun would be burned to a crisp in a fraction of a second."

"We'll take care of that," said the Frenchman. "We'll land him at night."

965.   When the first two mice were launched in space during the early years of space experimentation, one mouse said to the other: "I'm scared. It's dangerous you know, this space travel."

The second mouse replied: "Yeah, but it sure beats cancer research."

966.   An instructor was sitting on a bench on the campus one day when a space ship landed and a fantastic-looking creature came out. It had two heads with a single eye in the center of each. It had one arm growing out of the center of its chest and it walked with flippers.

"Earthling," the weird creature from outer space said, "Take me to your leader."

"Are you kidding," the instructor replied. "What you want to see is a plastic surgeon."

P

Parenthood (See Children, Men & Women, Motherhood, Students, Teenagers)

967.   A father summed up the problems of parenthood by explaining, "My oldest is in college and my youngest in nursery school. Some days you can hardly tell the difference."

968.   Irate father: "I sacrificed everything I had so you could go to school and study medicine—and now you tell me that I have to quit smoking."

969.   (Upon leaving a PTA meeting)
Twenty years ago I was told I wasn't as smart as my father. Today I'm told I'm not as smart as my teenage boy. Where did we go wrong?

970.   The two most difficult careers in life that are entrusted to amateurs are Citizenship and Parenthood.

971.   Did you hear about the counselor who fainted when his son asked for the garage keys and came out with the lawn mower.

972.   Parents are one of the hardships of a student's life.

973.   Did you hear about the father who was lecturing his son: "When I went to school," he said "I walked five miles a day."
"Yeah?" was the reply. "And what were you protesting?"

974.   "Sure, I'd like to have children some day, but I wouldn't want to be—well, you know—a parent."

975.   Planned Parenthood could be called "kid-mapping."

976.   Any student can tell you what's wrong with today's parents. They (the parents) think they know more than their children.

977.   Insanity has been proven to have been inherited. Parents get it from their children.

978. Parents these days scarcely bring up children; they finance them.

—John Brooks

979. Two professors met for lunch and were talking about the world problems, high taxes, the cost of living and finally about their own families.

"I have six boys," one of them said proudly.

"That's a nice family," sighed the other man, "I wish to heaven I had six children."

"Don't you have any children?" the other father asked with a touch of sympathy in his voice.

"Oh, yes," sighed the other man. "12."

980. Wife to reluctant husband who is helping their small son with his homework: "Help him now while you can. Next year he goes into fourth grade."

—*Akron Beach Journal* (Robert E. Wilson)

981. Planned parenthood is when the kids tell you what time you can use the car.

982. Willie had just received an "A" for the map of Europe that he had drawn.

"Willie," said his teacher, "this map is excellent! Did anyone help you do it?"

"Oh, no, Miss White," said Willie.

"Come, now, tell me the truth. Didn't your father help you?"

"No, Miss White," said Willie. "My father didn't help me. He did it all by himself."

—Skill Development Council, Inc.

983. Parenthood is hereditary—if your parents didn't have any children, chances are you won't either.

984. A budget, a little girl told her teacher, is when parents get mad and won't speak to each other.

985. Parents include women who yearn for that school girl complexion and men who long for that school boy digestion.

Peace (See Military)

986. Chief Rainwater say: "Everyone is smoking the pipe of peace, but no one is inhaling it."

987. When a man finds no peace within himself, it is useless to seek it elsewhere.

People (See Adult Education, Children, Mankind, Men & Women, Parenthood, Students, Youth)

988. The man who invented the eraser had the human race pretty well sized up.
>   —Phyl Anderson in the *New Glarus Post*

989. There are said to be two classes of people in the world; those who constantly divide the people of the world into two classes and those who do not.

990. People, like boats, toot the loudest when they are in a fog.

991. No two people are alike, and both of them are glad of it.
>   *—Morgan Square and Crescent*

992. There are three kinds of people: those who make things happen, those who watch things happen, and those who don't know what's happening.
>   —Longfellow

Perfection (See Ability, Genius, Self-Improvement)

993. Perfection is not attained at that point at which nothing can be added, but at that point at which nothing can be taken away.

994.   Perfection consists not in doing extraordinary things, but in doing ordinary things extraordinarily well.

—Antoine Arnauld

Philosophy (See American, Education, Mankind, Men & Women, Psychology)

995.   Student to Philosopher: "What do you think of culture in U.S.A.?"

Philosopher: "I'm in favor of it."

996.   All philosophy lies in two words: sustain and abstain.

—Epictetus

997.   Henry Ford's philosophy was that there is no dead end. "There is always a way out," he said. "What you learn in one failure, you utilize in your next."

998.   Philosophers, it is said, are intellectuals who talk about something they don't understand and make you think it is your fault.

Plays (See Dramatics, Movies, Theater)

999.   The eighth grade periodically staged "Romeo and Juliet" and "Macbeth."

In the seventh grade one day, the teacher asked who Shakespeare was.

"Oh, yeah," said one bright boy. "He's the guy who writes all those eighth-grade plays."

1000.   Drama Teacher: "Now before we start working on our class play, tell me have any of you had any stage experience."

David: "Once I had my leg in a cast."

Poise (See Manners, Tact)

1001.   Poise is the ability to talk fluently while the other teacher is paying the check.

1002.   Poise is like a duck—calm and unruffled on the surface but paddling as fast as possible underneath.

Politics (See America, Government)

1003.   Professor: "I don't really mind you marrying that young politician, but he doesn't stand too high in the political world."
Daughter: "Oh, yes he does. He already has been investigated by five different committees."

Prejudice (See Education, Teachers)

1004.   The difference between a prejudice and a conviction is that you can explain a conviction without getting mad.

1005.   There are still those who feel that the peoples of the world, though differing widely, can somehow learn to live together. After all, men and women do.

1006.   Many persons who boast of their open-mindedness are like the teacher who said as she went off to a meeting: "I'm not prejudiced at all. I am going with a perfectly open and unbiased mind to listen to what I am convinced is pure rubbish."

—The Curtis Courier

Principal (See Board-of-Education, School Teachers)

1007.   Principal: "When I retire I want to be superintendent of an orphans' home so I won't get letters from parents."

1008.   In the old days, if a youngster was in the principal's office, it meant the youngster was in trouble. Now it means the principal's in trouble.

—The Atlanta Constitution

1009.   The best principal is the one who has sense enough to pick good teachers to do what he wants done and self restraint to keep from meddling while they do it.

Problems (See Discipline, Mistakes, Misfortune)

1010. No problem is so big or so complicated that it can't be run away from.

1011. Problems are only opportunities in work clothes.

1012. Student at fraternity party: "He tried to drown his troubles, but found they were all excellent swimmers."

1013. Reading the papers, you realize that the old saying about the idle mind being the devil's workshop is all too true.

Everywhere, people who have shirts on their backs, food in their bellies and roofs over their heads are knee deep in trouble of their own making.

It just goes to show that if people ain't got problems, they'll make 'em, particularly if they have nothing else to do.

—Piney Woods Pete

Professors (See College, School, Teachers)

1014. Professors are people who go to college and never get out.

1015. College professors are men who get what's left after the football coach gets paid off.

1016. Professor: "If there are any morons in the room, please stand!"

After a long pause, a freshman rose. "And do you consider yourself a moron," commented the professor.

Student: "No sir. But I hate to see you standing alone."

Psychiatry (See Medicine, Mental Health, Psychology)

1017. During a lecture on psychopathology, a student raised his hand to ask a question. "Professor, you've told us about the abnormal person and his behavior, but what about the normal person?"

"If we ever find him," answered the Professor, "we'll cure him."

1018. Be a good psychiatrist and all the world will beat a psychopath to your door.

1019. The psychiatrist is the last man you talk to before talking to yourself.

1020. A psychiatrist is a man who will listen to you as long as you don't make sense.

1021. "The psychiatrist writing in the Alumni Journal said mothers ought to spend more time with their children," said the wife.

"Hmph," muttered the husband. "Sounds like he's just trying to drum up business."

1022. The professor told the story to his class about the young psychiatrist who was exhausted. Listening to the troubles of his patients all day left him worn, rumpled and depressed. As he got into the elevator to go home one night, he noticed an elderly colleague who looked fresh, dapper and full of energy. Wondering whether he had lost many patients, the younger man asked:

"How are things with you, Doctor?"

"Fine," said the veteran. "Had one of my busiest days today."

The young doctor was amazed. "But sir, how do you do it? After listening all day to troubles and complaints, how can you be so fresh and cheerful?"

"Who listens?" was the reply.

1023. Professor in psychiatry before beginning his lecture: "May I have your tension please."

1024. Mother of small boy to psychiatrist: "Well, I don't know whether he feels insecure, but everybody else in the neighborhood certainly does!"

Psychology (See Education, Mental Health, Psychiatry, Teachers)

1025. Seeing an attractive girl sitting alone in the cocktail lounge, a college student approached her politely and offered to buy her a drink.

"A motel!" she shrieked.

"No, no," he said embarrassed, "I said a drink . . . "

"You expect me to go to a motel with you?" she shrieked louder.

Daunted, the young man fled to the dim rear booth of the lounge to avoid the stares of other persons. A few minutes later, the girl came back to where he was seated and said softly. "I'd like to apologize for making you so uncomfortable at the bar. You see, I'm studying psychology at the university and I wanted to study the reactions of the people here."

To which the young student replied in a resounding roar, "Seventy-five dollars!"

1026. A psychologist believes a man shouldn't keep too much to himself. And so does Uncle Sam's Bureau of Internal Revenue.

PTA (See Kindergarten, Parenthood, School)

1027. Did you hear about the Hollywood youngster who was very proud because he had the most parents at the PTA meeting?

1028. PTA mothers outnumbered fathers three to one, so the president said, "We've got to stop meeting like this."

—Changing Times

1029. First Mother: "How are your children doing in school?"

Second Mother: "Better, but I still go to PTA meetings under an assumed name."

1030. A boy recently met his father at the door and said, "Dad, I'm supposed to tell you about a small PTA meeting tomorrow night."

"Since it's a small meeting, do I have to go?" the father asked.

"Guess so," replied the son. "It's just for you, me and the principal."

—Bob Stanely in the *Columbus Journal-Republican*

1031. The other day, my ten-year-old son brought home a notice from school, announcing a forthcoming PTA meeting. It was probably one of the most effective PTA notices ever mimeographed. It read:

See Mother run

See Father run

See Mother and Father run to the PTA meeting

See Mother and Father meet the pretty teacher
See Father smile
Tuesday night 8 p.m.

—F.L. Klinger in *Readers' Digest*

1032. A mother who has been through parent-teacher conferences from kindergarten through high school has her own particular hang-up.

Neither daughter No. 1 nor daughter No. 2 likes to speak up in class. Over the years, in evaluating the situation, teachers have volunteered such remarks as "Of course, their father doesn't talk much either," and occasionally, even their uncle's quiet nature has been brought into the conversation, too.

Slightly battle weary from having been on the receiving end of the same message for so many years now that daughter No. 2 is now a junior, she finally said to the teacher: "Well, you wouldn't want me to destroy the family image, would you?"

1033. As a motivator to encourage children to urge their parents to attend PTA meetings a school had a plaque that was displayed in the classroom that had the most parents the previous PTA meeting.

A teacher asked all of her students to write to their parents urging them to attend a meeting. One wrote: "Dear Mom and Dad. Please come to the PTA meeting tonight to help us bring back the plague."

R

Reading (See Books, English, Library, Words)

1034. Teaching people how to read is a lot easier than teaching them what to read.

1035. The growing popularity of speed reading should be a boon to the nation. For one thing, there will be fewer men blundering into the Ladies Room.

1036. Little Mary, a first grader, was listening intently as her older brother talked with a couple of friends about the merits of college.

The conversation turned to the average student's inability to read quickly. They exchanged helpful hints on the subject for several minutes. Finally, she decided to add her own advice to the conversation. She announced gravely, "Well, I've found that you can read a lot faster if you don't stop to color the pictures."

—Dan Bennett

1037.　　　The new teacher asked one of her students if he could read.
"Kinda," said the boy.
"What do you mean, kinda?"
"When I get to the crossroads," the boy explained, "I can tell how far, but I can't tell where to."

1038.　　　The town handyman had never learned to read, and that fact was of great concern to the school principal for whom he had sometimes done gardening. At last, he persuaded him to learn to read and he asked one of the local teachers to teach him.

Some months went by before the principal saw the handyman, and when he did, he said, "Well, Lester, I suspect by now you are able to read the Bible with some ease?"

"God bless ya, Sir, and thankee," he replied. "I was out of the Bible and inta th' racing form two weeks ago."

1039.　　　Look at a page of sheet music. If you have not been trained in music, what do those bars, staffs, clefs, notes, rests, sharps and flats mean to you? Nothing. They are mute. They are neither pretty or ugly. What matters is what they represent; what matters is the sound that can be unlocked by each of these little marks, the thrilling, inspiring harmony and power that can be released from the page by the musician who can interpret these little scribblings.

So it is with books. They are loaded with little groups of marks, pages of little marks, that are nothing in themselves. But these marks, too, are keys with which gates may be opened onto entire new and glowing worlds. Let us know how to read and teach all to read, and above all, let us read.

—*Nuggets*

1040.　　　Student: "Don't bother me. I'm writing to my girl friend."
Fellow Student: "But why write so slow?"
First Student: "Because she can't read very fast, that's why."

1041. Reading is one of our bad habits. . . . we read, most of the time, not because we wish to instruct ourselves, not because we long to have our feelings touched and our imagination fired, but . . . because we have time to spare.

—Aldous Huxley

1042. Speed reading is necessary these days or you'll never get off the freeway.

Report Card (See Education, School, Teachers)

1043. A little boy ran into the house, jumped across the bed, turned over the television, and jumped on the kitchen table.
"Mama! Mama!" he called, "I made an A in school."
"In what?" asked his mother.
"Self-control," said the son.

1044. Son: "Why do you always sign my report card with an X, Pop?"
Father: "With grades like yours, I'd just as soon your teacher didn't think your father can read or write."

1045. The boy walked unhesitantly up to his father. "Dad, here is my report card," he said, "and here also is an old one of yours that I found in the attic."

1046. Small boy, showing teacher's report card to his father: "Well, they're not paying her enough, for one thing."

1047. After the 14-year-old gloatingly turned up his father's old report card, Dad looked at it for a moment and then announced: "Well, son, you are right. This old report card of mine isn't any better than yours. I guess the only fair thing to do is to give you what my father gave me."

1048. Father, after checking his son's report card: "There's one thing in your favor. With these grades, you couldn't possibly be cheating."

1049. "What are these C's and D's on your report card?" shouted Dad to Junior.

"They're vitamin grades," replied Junior, without batting an eye.

1050. "Let's hope you show well in the ratings," the television star told his son as the boy presented his report card.

"Sorry, dad," replied the lad. "They want to sign me up to do another thirteen weeks this summer."

—Daphne Brown in the *Wall Street Journal*

1051. Linda to parents: "Here's my report card—and I'm tired of watching television anyway."

1052. The teacher asks why the little boy had not brought back his report card. "I got three A's this month and it's being circulated among my relatives."

1053. Father to mother: "At least this report card proves he isn't taking any mind-expanding drugs."

1054. Boy handing report card to parent: "Look this over and see if I can sue for defamation of character."

1055. Son, handing report card to his father: "Remember, Dad, they just print the bad news."

1056. Teacher: "Why are you painting your report card with luminous paint?"

Student: "I promised my mom and dad a glowing report."

1057. Father: "It's too bad they don't give a grade for courage. You'd get an 'A' just for bringing home this card."

Right (See Behavior, Education, Traits)

1058. To be right occasionally is not enough; a stopped clock is right twice a day.

To be right half the time is not so great; your lowly feet are right half the time.

Meanwhile, no one has ever found out how it would be to be right all the time.

1059. Right is might, but a good right never hurt a defender.

1060. Doing is the great thing. For if resolutely, people do what is right, in time they come to like doing it.

—Ruskin

1061. If you would convince a man that he does wrong, do right. Men will believe what they see. Let them see.

—Thoreau

Rumors (See Teachers)

1062. Rumors spread like butter. Ever try to *unspread* butter?

1063. When it comes to spreading rumors, it seems like the female of the species is much faster than the male.

1064. A rumor is often something negative that is then developed and enlarged.

1065. A rumor is something that isn't safe to repeat but is often juicy to hear.

S

Satisfaction (See Friendship, Happiness)

1066. Few things in life are more satisfying than parking on what's left of the other fellow's nickel.

—*The Adams County Times*

1067. In attempting to illustrate satisfaction to his class, the teacher cited this story:

A Quaker put up a sign on a vacant piece of ground next to his house: "I will give this lot to anyone who is really satisfied."

A wealthy farmer, as he rode by, read it. Stopping, he said: "Since he is going to give the piece of land away, I may as well have it as anyone else. I am rich, I have all I need, so I am able to qualify." He went to the door.

"Are you really satisfied?" asked the Quaker.

"Yes," said the farmer. "I have all I need and am well satisfied."

"Friend," said the other, "if you are satisfied, what do you want with my lot?"

1068. "It doesn't do any good to complain to the janitor about our cold classrooms," said one teacher to another.

"Oh, yes it does," said the other. "I get all warmed up when I shout at him."

1069. "And if I take this teaching job, is it possible to get an increase in salary every year?"

"Yes, provided your work is satisfactory."

"Oh, I thought there was a catch to it somewhere."

School (See College, Diploma, Education, Faculty Meetings, High School, Kindergarten, PTA, Students, Teachers, Tradition)

1070. One day the teacher told her class that from now on she would ask a special question every Friday. The pupil who answered the question correctly wouldn't have to return to school until the following Tuesday.

Next Friday, the teacher asked the class a difficult question. As expected, no one could answer it.

The following Friday, one of the boys brought a rubber ball to class. At the time for the special question to determine if anyone would get a day off from school the next week, Johnny tossed the rubber ball to the front of the room.

"Whose ball is this?" questioned the teacher.

"Mine!" Johnny answered. "See you next Tuesday."

—David Wenzel
Boy's Life

1071. "Life is sure a put-down," Nona sighed sadly.

"What do you mean?" asked her friend. "Did something happen?"

"No," she said. "It's just that last year in third grade I was one of the big kids at Hillcrest. And this year, in fourth grade I'm one of the little kids at Marquette."

—Kewanunee Enterprise

1072. "Did you ever attend a school for stammering?"

"No, I just pi-pi-picked it up."

1073. "Isn't Fall a wonderful time of the year? New TV programs, the kids are back to school, all the highway detours are fixed, too early to shovel snow and not much grass mowing."

—Stan Ihlenfeldt
Elkhorn Independent

1074. Adam and Eve invented the first loose-leaf system.

1075. The teacher sent Bobby home with a note to his mother that suggested that she give her son a bath.

The next day, Bobby arrived in class with a note from his parent.

"Der Miz Smith," said the note. "Bobby comes to school to git learnt, not smelt. He ain't no rose."

1076. A very dejected little boy came home from school on his first day at school.

"Ain't goin' tomorrow," he said.

"Why?" asked his mother.

"Well, I can't read 'n write 'n they won't let me talk, so what's the use?"

1077. "Daddy, I need 50 cents to take to school today."

"What for?"

"My teacher's resigning and we're raising money to give her a little momentum."

1078.   School boards have a tough time these days—monitoring the length of girls' dresses and of boys' hair, fighting, and guarding them against catching religion.

—Smiles

1079.   During recess, the school principal was approached by a pupil whom he recognized to be the daughter of the local minister.

"Sir," the child began. "Johnny Smith said a bad word to me on the playground."

"Well, we'll see about that!" declared the principal.

"What did he say?"

"Oh," replied the girl, "my daddy doesn't let me use such language but if you'll say all the naughty words you know, I'll stop you when you come to it."

—F.G. Kernan

1080.   One mother confiding to another: "My kid's been uneasy about starting back to school this term. He got the summer job one of his teachers wanted."

1081.   School is the mouse race that equips you for the rat race.

1082.   Russian children go to school six days a week. This can never happen in America because Saturday is the day teachers wash their hair.

1083.   I'm told that a pair of brothers, first graders, came home from school the other day.

"Mother," said one "what does G-I-R-L-S spell?"

"It spells girls," the mother said.

The boy turned to his brother and said accusingly. "See? I told you we were in the wrong room."

1084.   One of our staff members reports that his son came home from school the other day to inform his mother that his school is sponsoring a bake and rummage sale.

"I know you can bake a cake," he told his mother "but do we have any old rummages?"

1085.   Most public schools have rules against dispensing any kind of medication, even aspirin, that has led to the utterance of an educational epigram.

"Schools have the right to give you a headache, but not to give aspirins to cure them."

1086.   School days can be the happiest days of a mother's life—provided she has a child old enough to go to school.

1087.   From a bumper sticker on a schoolbus:
"School Used To Be Fun. Now It's A Riot."

1088.   Father: "What's your favorite subject in school?"
Son: "I guess gozinta."
Father: "What's gozinta—a new language?"
Son: "Naw, just gozinta . . . two gozinta four, four gozinta eight, eight gozinta sixteen!"

1089.   School kids used to listen to the radio to learn whether their schools had been closed due to weather conditions. Now they listen to learn whether the schools are closed because the teachers are on strike.

—Pittsburgh Post Gazette

1090.   In July school has been out long enough to make most mothers proponents of the 12 month school plan.

1091.   "It was a little easier to get through school in my day. The questions were just as hard, but praying was still legal."

—Bob Hope in the *Family Weekly*

1092.   "Remember the good old days when a student would write home: 'Dear Dad, got an A in business management, send money for laundry.' Today they say: 'Flunked picketing, mail bail.' "

—Bob Hope in the *Family Weekly*

1093.   A youngster wrote to the Library of Congress: "I am no help to my teachers because I have no research information. I would appreciate it very much if you could send me anything about anything."

1094.   Teacher: "You got excused because you said your grandma was dying. Today, I saw her in the beauty parlor."
Student: "That's where she was dyeing. Now she's a blonde."

–Timothy Scheid
Boy's Life

1095.   "When the teacher asked a question I was the first to raise my hand," the boy told his father.
"Then why didn't you get better marks?"
"Because by the time I got back to the classroom somebody else had already answered the question."

1096.   Concerned about the maintenance of his school's newly-painted walls, the custodian had this sign posted:
"This is a partition, not a petition. No signatures required."

1097.   Teacher: "Will someone please name the four seasons?"
Johnny: "Salt, pepper, sugar, spice."

1098.   Sign on school blackboard during exams: "Do your own think."

1099.   Notice on school bulletin board: "In case of atomic attack the Federal ruling against praying in this school will be temporarily suspended."

1100.   Sign in cloakroom at the University above a row of hooks: "For Faculty Members Only."
Underneath someone wrote: "May also be used for hats and coats."

1101.   You can't expect any school to give you anything unless you bring something to put into it.

1102. Woman's Page Item: Mr. and Mrs. Fred Smith were married on Saturday, ending a friendship which began during their years at Park High School.

1103. A student transferred from one public school in another state and her teacher was interested in finding what basic reader she had used.
"In your school," asked the teacher "did you read about Dick and Jane?"
"Yes," replied the child "but in our book Dick is Jerry and Jane is Mary."

School Administration

1104. Said the newly-hired secretary in the Dean's office: "Do you want double-spacing on the carbons, too, sir?"

1105. After careful investigation, the new university clerk found thousands and thousands of old documents in the files, none of which served any purpose whatsoever. He promptly applied to the superintendent of the department to burn them.
After two months, back came the answer: "Yes, but be careful to make copies of the documents first, and see that the copies are carefully filed.
—Smiles

1106. Swamped with work, the Dean called his switchboard operator, "Look, Miss Jones, don't put through any calls to me this morning. I'll be incommunicado."
"Well, all right," she replied. "But in case anything important comes up, hadn't you better let me have your number there."

School Board (See Schools, Teachers)

1107. A county school board in Michigan wrote this sentence for us to decipher:
"With the exception of vehicles approaching the stopped school bus with red flashers activated, it is a wise procedure for all motorists to stop when coming upon a stopped school bus with red flashers activated."

School Bus (See Schools, etc.)

1108. School Bus Driver: A man who thought he liked children.

1109. An ironworker was nonchalantly walking the beam, high above the street on a new skyscraper.

When he came down, a man who had been watching him, tapped his shoulder. "I was amazed at your calmness up there. How did you happen to go to work on a job like this?"

"Well," said the iron worker, "I used to drive a school bus but my nerves gave out."

1110. The family overslept, and their six-year-old missed the school bus.

Her father, though late for work, agreed to drive her to school if she would direct him.

They drove several blocks before she told him to turn, then many more blocks before she indicated another turn.

This went on for twenty minutes. Finally they reached the school which proved to be only a five minute drive from their home.

Asked why she had directed him by such a circuitous route, the child explained: "That's the way the school bus goes."

—Dan Bennett in *Family Weekly*

Science (See Biology, Botany, Chemistry, Nature Study, Zoology)

1111. Science Teacher: "When water becomes ice, what is the greatest change that takes place?"

Bright Student: "The price!"

1112. One thing we know about the speed of light—it gets here early in the morning.

1113. Scientists have now invented a complicated "thought machine" so sensitive that it already has a stomach ulcer.

1114. Science Prof: "What happens when a body is immersed in water?"

Coed: "Either the doorbell or the telephone rings."

1115. Science has been taking great strides forward. Now it's only 50 years behind the comic books.

1116. Professor Hidome, a specialist in hybridizing things, once crossed a crocodile with an abalone. He was endeavoring to get an "abadile." Instead, he got a "croc-o-balone."

1117. A teacher was demonstrating a science experiment on air pressure for her upper primary class.

Using a vacuum pump, she exhausted air from a gallon can and the class watched the can collapse.

One deeply impressed boy asked her if she had learned to do that in college: "Yes," she answered.

"No wonder it took four years!" responded the student.

1118. Teacher: "Tommy, make up a sentence using the word 'climate.'"

Tommy: "The mountain was so big that I could not climate."

1119. A science teacher was giving his class a demonstration on the harm of alcohol. He took two jars, one filled with alcohol and one filled with water. Next he took a worm and dipped it in the water and the worm swam about.

Then he dipped the worm in the alcohol and the worm died. The teacher then asked a small boy in the room what this lesson had proved. The lad explained, "If you drink enough alcohol, you won't have worms."

1120. A "fact" is anything that hasn't been proven wrong.

1121. The trouble with science today is that it is slowly filling our homes with appliances that are smarter than the people who live in them.

1122. A peeping Tom is a doubting Thomas doing research.

1123. If science can ever cross a parrot with a black panther, you'd better listen when it talks.

Self-Improvement (See Education)

1124. When the average person talks about "bettering himself," he means a higher salary, not self-improvement.

Service (See Education, Teaching)

1125. Professor: "I used to be a self-made man, but now I'm only a remodeling project engineered by a wife and daughter."

1126. Seeing cold cream on her mother's face for the first time, the little girl stared at her with a puzzled expression. The mother explained that she used the cream to make herself pretty.

The child watched as her mother removed the cream with tissues. Then looking closely at her she sighed and said, "It didn't help any, did it?"

1127. Salesman (to farmer): "Now that your son is going to school, he should have an encyclopedia?"

Farmer: "Not on your life. Let him walk like I did."

Service (See Education, Teaching)

1128. He who serves his country well has no need of ancestors.

—Francois M. Voltaire

1129. A man cannot leave a better legacy to the world than a well-educated family.

—Thomas Scott

1130. Ask not what my country can do for me but what I can do for my country.

—John F. Kennedy

Sex Education (See Education, Homework, Love, Men, Men & Women)

1131. The Dean of Women at a girl's college was lecturing her students on the subject of sex. "In moments of temptation," she said, "ask yourself one question—is an hour of pleasure worth a lifetime of shame?"

A demure young girl in the back of the room spoke up and asked: "Tell me, Dean, how do you make it last an hour?"

1132. There is a lot of talk lately about sex education in schools. Suppose that is one course in which parents might do a little worrying if their junior high student DOES get an A.

—Larry Arnold in the *Juneau County Chronicle*

1133. Remember when the only time you asked "Is it a boy or girl?" was at the hospital.

1134. The battle of sexes has lost some of its steam since it's difficult to tell who's which.

1135. At a teachers' convention luncheon recently the speeches were running overly long. Finally, the toastmaster rose to introduce the last speaker, saying:

"I know you are all anxious to hear our next guest, the distinguished sociologist from our university, but it's getting late and I've asked the doctor to make his speech as brief as possible. As you know he is going to talk to us on 'sex.' "

The good doctor rose, glanced around the table and said: "Gentlemen, it gives me great pleasure." Then he sat down.

1136. A seven-year-old daughter came home from school one day with a long face.

"We had a test in school," she told her mother "and I got an F in sex."

The mother was speechless. "I didn't know they were teaching sex education in her school," she said later "and I couldn't believe that if they were, she could get an F. We've answered her questions on the subject so carefully."

When she got her voice back, the mother started questioning her daughter and learned that the F was in a little box after the word "sex" at the beginning of the test along with her name, age and grade in school.

"Honey," the mother told her daughter happily, "that F just means you're a girl."

1137. A 70-year-old friend says that sex, as far as he is concerned, consists entirely of futility rights.

Speaking (See Introductions, Spelling, Teachers, Words)

1138. Some speakers electrify an audience—others gas it.

1139. The easiest way to stay awake during a one-hour lecture is to deliver it.

1140.   Oratory is the art of making sounds deep in the chest like important messages from the brain.

1141.   Lecturing is the art of delivering a two-minute idea with a two hour vocabulary.

1142.   Usually, the best way to save face is by keeping the lower half shut.

1143.   The best audience is one that is intelligent, well-educated—and a little drunk.

1144.   A student recognized one of her professors in a hotel pacing up and down in a preoccupied manner. Quietly, she asked why he was there.
"I'm about to deliver a speech in a few minutes," he said.
"Are you always nervous before making a speech to the public," she asked.
"Oh no," he said. "I never get nervous."
"Then what," she wanted to know, "are you doing in the Ladies' Powder Room?"

—College Laughs

1145.   Be blunt and you won't be thought to be dull.

1146.   A professor was handed a note by his wife just as he was about to deliver an after-dinner speech.
The note, at first glance, read "KISS."
He was thinking of how nice this was of his wife when he noticed the smaller letters. When read carefully, the note said:
"Keep It Short Stupid!"

1147.   Don't know which speaker is harder to listen to—the fellow who never quits or the fellow who never quips.

1148.   Bill: "What follows our lecturer?"
Mac: "Tomorrow."

1149.　　　When holding a conversation, be sure to let go of it once in awhile.

1150.　　　The graduation ceremony was over and the principal and his wife were home relaxing before preparing for bed. "What did you think of my speech today," he asked her.

"Well, dear, "replied the wife, "you got off one thing that made me very proud."

"What was that?" he asked.

"The stage."

1151.　　　Remember always that your tongue is in a wet place and likely to slip.

Spelling (See English, Teachers, Words)

1152.　　　Dictionary—A guide to the spelling of words which can be located if you know how to spell them.

1153.　　　It was open school week and the proud mother was speaking to the teacher. "My child is a genius. He has many original ideas, doesn't he?"

"Oh yes," replied the teacher, "especially when it comes to spelling."

1154.　　　Teacher: "How do you spell 'melancholy'?"

Student: "The same as everyone else."

1155.　　　Sign on a college bulletin board offering student services: "Excellent, fast typing of term papers. Good Speler."

Sports (See Baseball, Basketball, Football)

1156.　　　Rowing Coach: "So you want to come out for the crew. Ever rowed before?"

Freshman: "Only a horse, Sir."

1157.　　　A Russian track coach, interviewed by an American sportswriter, was asked why the Soviets are now producing such fast runners.

"It's quite simple," he explained. "In our starting guns we use real bullets."

1158.   We're in the short week period of the year now—Monday, Tuesday, Wednesday, Thursday, Football, Football, Football.
—Stan Ihlenfeldt in the *Elkhorn
Independent*

1159.   A short fellow discussed his tennis game with a friend. "When my opponent hits the ball to me, my brain immediately barks out a command to my body: 'Race to the net'—it says, 'slam a blistering drive to the far corner, jump back into position to return the next volley.' "
"Then?" asked his friend.
"Then," sighed the rotund one, "my body says, 'Who—me?' "

1160.   Principal: "How's Jones on the high jump? Any good?"
Coach: "Terrible! He can hardly clear his throat!"

1161.   The basketball player rushed into his history class ten minutes late. "I hate to be late," he panted to a classmate. "But I need the sleep."

1162.   Saturday golfers are fugitives from dirty basements and long lawn grass.

Students (See College, Education, High School, Juvenile Delinquent, Kindergarten, School, Teenagers)

1163.   Maybe students wouldn't be so objectionable if they shaved.

1164.   Advertisement in personal column of college newspaper: "Sweet old lady wishes to correspond with young male student, preferably her son."

1165.   Teenagers today know *everthing*—except the lessons the teacher assigned to them for tomorrow's school day.

1166. A college student had been pestering his father for a new car. On a visit to the campus, the parent pointed out that most of the cars in the parking lot were quite old.

"But dad," the youth protested, "those cars belong to the faculty."

1167. "I think my son must be home from college?" said the mother.

"You think he is? Don't you know?" said her neighbor.

"Only on circumstantial evidence," replied the mother. "He hasn't written home for money in three weeks, and the car is missing."

1168. Harassed surgeon to medical students watching a delicate operation: "Will the wise guy who keeps saying 'oops' please leave!"

1169. The "professional student" is a fellow who thinks he should approach life's realities cautiously, by degrees.

1170. When asked about his "C" in conduct, the little boy replied: "I guess I just don't know how to do that."

1171. "I'm sending you the $10 you requested in your last letter," wrote the businessman to his son in college. "However, I'm surprised that at your educational level you haven't learned to be more careful with your spelling. There was one error in your letter that I must call to your attention. The figure "10" is written with one nought, not two."

1172. Student: "Dad, you're a lucky man."
Father: "How come?"
Student: "You won't have to buy me any college books this year. I have to repeat three of my courses next semester."

1173. The student who spends too much time at the local bar will find his education lacking, to a degree.

1174. Engineering students are baffled by the fact that often the girls with the most streamlined shapes offer the most resistance.

1175. "What does your boy plan to be when he graduates from college?"

"I'm not really sure," replied the father, "but judging from his letters, he'll end up a professional fund raiser."

1176. A scheduled. campus demonstration was suddenly called off when it was discovered none of the students present could play the guitar.

1177. Our daughter went to college,
The reason you can guess;
Not to earn her Ph D,
But to get her MRS.
—Rosa Lee Lloyd in the *Wall Street Journal*

1178. College kids of well-to-do parents have found a way to save more money—they fly home as "Mr. and Mrs."

1179. Nearing the end of the long trail to a medical degree, a student wrote home: "The closer I am to the practice of medicine, the more I realize how little I actually know, and the thought scares me. In fact 95 per cent of my class feels the same way, and the rest are going to be psychiatrists."

1180. There's a great deal of talk about apathy in our universities. So 1,000 students were asked if they were apathetic; 44 said "yes," 69 said "no" and 887 had no opinion.

1181. In this day of advanced degrees, two fathers were discussing the problem of putting a boy through college. Said one: "What is your son going to be when he finishes his education?"

The other replied glumly, "An octogenarian, I think."

1182. A boy in Junior High School was having trouble with some of his science homework. So he began popping into his father's study to ask questions. Each time, the father would lower his newspaper to his lap, listen thoughtfully to the question, ponder for a moment, and then say, "I'm sorry, son, I'm afraid I don't know the answer to that one."

After many repetitions of that exchange, the boy started to ask another question, then decided against it, saying, "Oh, Dad, never mind!"

"Come on, Son," insisted the father. "After all, you never learn anything if you don't ask."

—Nuggets

1183. It is generally not wise to push a bright child through school too fast. He may arrive at college too young to use a razor.

1184. "I agree," the school principal said "that your son may have a spark of genius. But ... in my opinion, he also has ignition trouble."

1185. All a youngster wants out of school these days is himself.

1186. In reviewing the academic record of one of my students so that I could write her a letter of recommendation, I noticed that among many good grades she had also earned an F. Since she had achieved high grades in difficult subjects such as physics and philosophy, the F in physical education course seemed peculiar. "How did you manage to get an F in archery?" I asked.

She looked sheepish and replied, "I shot the teacher."

—Virginia Vandever in Readers' Digest

1187. A boy who was generally a poor student, one day startled his family by announcing that he was the only one in his class to get 100 in a Civic class test.

"That's wonderful," commented the father. "Were the questions hard?"

"Only one," answered the boy. "They asked us, how much is the salary of an Associate Justice of the United States Supreme Court? Well, I didn't know, but I figured that if a star pitcher on a baseball team was worth $140,000, an Associate Justice ought to be worth about a fourth as much. So I put down $35,000 and I was right."

1188. Teacher: "Which hand is the Statue of Liberty holding over her head?"

Smart Kid: "The one with the torch."

1189. Second Grader to Teacher: "In my prayers last night, I asked God to keep you well 'cause I don't want no substitutes."

1190. Teacher: "Iceland is the same size as Siam."
Student (writing in notebook): "Iceland is about the same size as my teacher."

1191. Modern student to teacher before exam: "Where can I plug in my electric eraser?"

1192. Student demands in previous generations were simple. In the classroom, they consisted of a finger extended in the air and an anxious look.

—Louis Pfugjoeft in the *Algoma Record-Herald*

1193. First college student: "You look all broken up. What's the matter?"
Second student: "I wrote home for money for a study lamp."
First student: "So, what's wrong with that?"
Second student: "They sent the lamp."

—Anna Herbert
Family Weekly

1194. Leo says that youngsters are like canoes. They go straighter when paddled from the rear.

1195. Revolting students sure are!

1196. When students dance nowadays, they don't talk, they don't touch one another, they don't even look at one another. It's like being married for 30 years.

—Tombstone (Ariz.) *Eptaph*

1197. A school boy can usually get well by Saturday . . . and a wage earner by payday.

1198. Our youngest grandson won't need an aptitude test when he starts school. Right now he's apt to do most anything.

1199. An underprivileged today is an American schoolboy without a portable typewriter.

1200. As U.S. 101 slowed through Santa Barbara, the row of flower children hitching rides was an amusing sight, but the most appealing was a bearded youth holding a sign which read: STUDENT—UNARMED.

1201. The freshman stood up to begin his speech. "Washington is dead," he began in a strong voice. "Lincoln is dead. . . ." Everything went blank. Then weakly—"and I . . . I'm beginning to feel a little sick myself."

1202. My son is quite a wrestler. He wrestles with the big shots. He wrote me from college that the dean had him on the carpet the other day.

1203. A student walked into his home looking very dejected.
"Didn't you make the debating team?" asked his mother.
"N-n-n-no," he replied. "They s-s-aid I wasn't t-t-t-tall enough."

1204. It's a fact that there are militant students even among those taking correspondence courses. One young man recently beat up his mailman.

1205. What this country needs are some colleges that teach everything that students think they already know.

1206. Sign on a schoolboy's book: "In case of flood, stand on this!"

Study (See Education, Homework, Students, Teachers)

1207. Proud father to mother as they watch their small son, lying on the floor studying by the light from the TV screen: "Reminds you of Abe Lincoln, doesn't it?"

Success (See Ability, Failure)

1208. Some people study all their life, and at their death they have learned everything except to think.

—Domergue

1209.
She has the TV going;
Her record player bleats.
And while she's telephoning,
She guzzles pop and eats.
Don't ask her any questions
To make her little dome work.
The child is in the process
Of getting through her homework!

—Georgie Starbuck Galbraith

1210. The more we study the more we discover our ignorance.

—Shelley

1211. The study of history is useful to the historian by teaching him his ignorance of women.

—Henry Brooks Adams

Success (See Ability, Failure)

1212. The road to success is always under construction.

1213. Success has been defined as "making mistakes while no one is looking."

1214. The recipe for success is the same as that for a nervous breakdown.

1215. You know you've arrived as a real success when your name appears in everything but the phone directory.

1216. The most difficult part of getting to the top of the ladder is getting through the crowd at the bottom.

—The Oakland (Neb.) *Independent*

1217. Someone once asked the French writer, Jean Cocteau, if he believed in luck.

"Certainly," he said. "How else do you explain success of those you don't like?"

1218. The dictionary is the only place where "success" comes before "work."

1219. If you don't know the price of success, the Internal Revenue Service will.

1220. The road to success is paved with good inventions.

1221. Any road to success can stand constant improvement.

1222. The mathematical formula for success in life is, "X plus Y plus Z, when X is work, Y is play, and Z is keep your mouth shut."

1223. The mama whale was instructing the baby whale in the facts of life. "Remember," she said "it's only when you get to the top and start to blow off steam that you get harpoons thrown at you."

1224. One trouble with the road to success is that we have to pave it ourselves.

1225. Success is only a matter of luck. Just ask any failure.

1226. Success has turned more heads than halitosis.

1227. "What is your formula for success?" the reporter asked the retiring multi-millionaire.

"I attribute all my success to my wife," was the reply.

"To her help and support?" prompted the reporter.

"Not that," replied the millionaire, "It was just that I was curious to know if there was any income she couldn't live beyond."

1228.   The key to success is the one that fits the ignition.

1229.   When you can think of yesterday without regret and of tomorrow without fear, you are on the road to success.

1230.   It's more difficult getting up in the morning when you're wearing silk pajamas.

—Eddie Arcaro

1231.   Success in life is measured less by I.Q. than by "I Will." Steadfastness of purpose, devotion to ideals and old-fashioned gumption will be as important to the world of tomorrow as they have been in the past. Like charity, they start at home.

1232.   God has given us two ends: one to sit on and one to think with. Success depends on which end we use the most—

Heads we win
Tails we lose.

1233.   Behind every successful man is someone who says he went to school with him.

1234.   Behind many successful men are women who said: "Go ahead stupid, you can do it."

Summer Employment (See Job Opportunities, Moonlighting, Students, Teachers)

1235.   A college teacher found his summer employment as a door-to-door salesman brought him a fund of stories as well as some ready cash.

He particularly found this true one day when his sales pitch had become routine. A boy opened the door to his knock, listened to him intently and then yelled inside, "Mom, there's a live commercial at the door!"

Sunday School Teaching

1236.   When a Sunday School teacher asked her class what they were thankful for, one eight-year-old boy replied, "My glasses."

"Why your glasses?" the teacher inquired.

"Well," he said "they keep the boys from fighting with me and keep the girls from kissing me."

—The Sunday School Times

1237. "Now children," said the Sunday School Teacher, "I've told you the story of Jonah and the whale. Willie, you may tell us what this story teaches."

Willie: "It teaches us that you can't keep a good man down."

1238. An eight-year-old lad was asked by his mother what he had learned at Sunday School.

"Well," he said, "Our teacher told us about when God sent Moses behind enemy lines to rescue the Israelites from the Egyptians. When they came to the Red Sea, Moses called for the engineers to build a pontoon bridge. After they had all crossed, they looked back and saw the Egyptian tanks coming. Moses radioed headquarters on his walkie-talkie to send bombers to blow up the bridge and saved the Israelities."

"Bobby!" exclaimed his mother. "Is that really the way your teacher told you the story?"

"Not exactly," he admitted. "But if I told it her way, you'd never believe it."

1239. "Now, how many of you would like to go to heaven?" asked the Sunday School teacher. All the eager four-year-olds raised their hands except Tommy.

"Don't you want to go to heaven, Tommy?" asked the teacher.

"I'm sorry, I can't. My mother told me to come right home after Sunday School."

1240. Two youngsters were walking home from Sunday School after having been taught a lesson about the devil. One of the boys said to the other. "What do you think about all that devil stuff?"

"Well," replied the other. "You know how Santa Claus turned out. It's probably just your dad."

1241. Sunday School teacher: "Timmy, why do you say God's home is not in heaven but in the bathroom of your house?"

Timmy: "Cause every morning my Pop knocks on the bathroom door and yells, 'My Lord, are you still in there?' "

1242.   The boy came home from Sunday School and told his mother that if he missed three Sundays in a row, his teacher was going to throw him into the furnace.

Horrified, the mother phoned the teacher.

"What I said," the teacher explained "was if any child missed three Sundays in a row he would be dropped from the register."

1243.   After listening to the story of Lot's wife looking back and being turned into a pillar of salt, the Sunday School youngster commented:

"My mother was driving the car one time when she looked back . . . and turned into a telephone pole."

T

Tact (See Diplomacy)

1244.   After a speech, a college president was approached by a little white-haired woman who told him how much she had enjoyed his talk. "I take the liberty to speak to you," she said, "because you told us you love old ladies."

"I do, I do," was the gallant reply, "and I also like them your age."

—Smiles

1245.   To explain "tact" to his students, the teacher told the story about the Army master sergeant who used the steamroller approach on every occasion. One day the captain called him in and told him that a telegram had come, he said, bearing the news of the death of Private O'Malley's grandmother. "I'm afraid you'll have to go out in the barracks and break the news to O'Mally, Sergeant," the captain said sadly.

"Yessir," replied the sergeant who then stepped to the door of the barracks and roared, "Hey, O'Malley! Yer grammaw just died."

The captain was horror-struck by the sergeant's crude technique in such matters, informed him that he must learn a little subtlety, and told him to report to the Army's School of Tact and Personnel Relations for six weeks' schooling. The sergeant went. He returned with his diploma six weeks later, just about the time a telegram arrived telling of the death of Private Lopez' grandmother.

"I'll take care of this Sir, *tactfully,*" said the sergeant. "Watch this." He went to the middle of the barracks and called the company to attention.

"Now," he commanded, "all men with living grandmothers take one step forward. Not so fast, Lopez!"

Teachers-Teaching (See College Education, High School, Professors, Students, Sunday School Teaching)

1246. A true teacher defends his pupils against his own personal influence.

—Bronson Alcott

1247. Note from teacher: "Mary is a good worker but she talks too much."
Reply from father: "You should come over and meet her mother."

1248. ·Ah, for the good old days when a teacher's strike landed on the seat of the pants!

1249. There's a teacher in our high school who is so ugly that the other night when a Peeping Tom chanced by her house *he* reached in and pulled down her shade.

1250. The-teacher walked into the noisy classroom, slapped his hand on the desk and ordered sharply, "I demand pandemonium." The class quieted down at once.

"It isn't what you ask," he bragged later in the teachers' lounge. "It's how you ask for for it."

1251. One grade school teacher received this note from a considerate mother: "I kept Junior home yesterday because he had a cold. What a peaceful day you must have had."

1252. A High School teacher displays the following sales pitch on his bulletin board: "FREE. Every Monday through Friday. Knowledge. Bring your own containers."

1253. "I don't want to scare you," the 7-year-old informed his teacher, "but my daddy says if I don't get better grades somebody's going to get spanked."

1254. The principal of the local junior high school heard shouting and laughter as he passed one room. He opened the door in time to see one long-haired youth shouting and dancing down the aisle. He seized the lad, dragged him into the corridor, and told him to stand there until excused.

Next the principal returned to the classroom and restored order. After giving a long lecture on discipline, he asked if there were any more questions.

"Yes," one student said. "When are you going to let our teacher come back in the room?"

1255. Lulu has just confessed that she wanted to be a school teacher, but she couldn't spell. So she became a secretary.

1256. A person too dumb to teach the ignorant isn't much value to our present day society.

1257. A professor who had taught for many years was counseling a young teacher.

"You will discover," he said "that in nearly every class there will be a youngster eager to argue. Your first impulse will be to silence him, but I advise you to think carefully before doing so. He probably is the only one listening."

1258. At a party a plump and kittenish woman cornered a young man, who tried desperately to escape.

"Do you remember the youngster who used to tickle you under the chin at school?" he asked.

"Well," she exclaimed. "I thought I recognized you. That's who you are."

"No Ma'am," he said. "That was my father."

1259. Despite the publicity about teaching machines and all, the third grade's Miss Jones is still the quoted authority on Pilgrims and all numbers over 12.

—Changing Times

1260. The child learns only from lovable teachers; he is not a man until he learns also from hateful teachers.

—Ivan Panin

1261. Professor to students: "Always use graduates instead of pipettes for measuring cyanide solutions. If you use pipettes, we'll not have any graduates."

1262. The teacher placed this sentence on the blackboard. "I didn't have no fun over the week-end."
"Now, how could I correct this," she asked her class.
Larry stood up and said, "Get yourself a date."

1263. One morning when I had many things on my mind, I continually called my students by incorrect names.
A heavy sigh came from the front row, followed by a thin, high voice. "Boy, you're all out of shape today."

—Catherine Newline, Elmira, N.Y.

1264. The nurse entered the professor's room and said softly, "It's a boy, sir."
The professor looked up from his desk.
"Well," he said "what does he want?"

1265. "Have you any abnormal children in your class?" a harassed-looking teacher was asked.
"Yes," she replied. "Two of them have good manners."

1266. A first grade teacher fresh from college was taking over her first class. Upon entering the classroom she noticed a nasty word on the blackboard followed by the signature, "Thrush."
So she said: "Now children, let's fold our hands, put them on our desks and put our heads down on the desks. Then the person who wrote this on the blackboard can come up and erase it."
So they folded their hands, put them on their desks and put their heads down on the desks. All was quiet for a while then there was a thump, thump of feet scurrying to the blackboard and back to the desk.

After everything was quiet again the teacher said. "Now let's see if the bad word is thoroughly erased." So they looked to see a new, nastier word. followed by "Thrush Strikes Again!"

1267. Beginning teacher's musing after the first week of school:
1. It is the teachers that will be taut.
2. Nothing succeeds like recess.
3. When a teacher teaches punctuation many of his students go into a coma.
4. At the end of a day, a teacher's grief case is full.

1268. At school one day Johnny's teacher found it necessary to leave the room. When she returned there was absolute silence.

"Well, well," she said. "Your behavior is a pleasant surprise."

Johnny raised his hand.

"What is it?" asked the teacher.

"You told us," said Johnny "that if you ever came back to the classroom and found us all sitting perfectly still and making no noise, you'd drop dead."

1269. A teaching sister applying for a passport paused pensively at the form that asked "Distinguishing Marks." Then with a twinkle in her eye, she wrote "Nun."

1270. Some parents are always trying to get teachers to give their kids special consideration. And now they're learning things from psychologists. I was having a talk with one mother about her son's bad behavior and she said: "Hit the boy next to him and this will frighten Melvin."

—Jack Martin

1271. I suppose if the classroom should be replaced by the TV screen, slow learners could always watch the reruns.

—Jack Martin

1272. The teacher was giving a lesson on magnets to her second graders. Afterwards, she asked questions. To one little boy, she said, "My name begins with an M and I pick up things, now tell me what I am."

The boy replied without even a bat of the eye, "You're a mother."

—Earl A. Mathes in the *Keil Tri-County Record*

1273.   There was the English teacher who regarded Santa's helpers as a bunch of subordinate clauses.

—Tom Worth
Boy's Life

1274.   If you make people think they're thinking, they'll love you; but if you really make them think, they'll hate you.

—Don Marquis

1275.   There was a teacher who graded so hard that he even took off for upside down periods.

1276.   *Why Teach?*
They ask me why I teach, and I reply:
"Where would I find more splendid company?
There sits a statesman,
Strong, unbiased, wise,
Another later Webster,
Silver-tongued,
And there a doctor
Whose quick, steady hand
Can mend a bone,
Or stem a lifeblood's flow.
A builder sits beside him—
Upward rise
The arches of a church he builds, wherein
That minister will speak the word of God,
And lead a stumbling sole to touch the Christ.
And all about a less gathering
Of farmers, merchants, teachers,
Laborers, men
Who work with man and vote and build
And plan and pray
Into a great tomorrow."
And I say,
"I may not see the church,
Or hear the words,
Or eat the food their hands will grow
And yet . . . . I may,"
And later I may say,
"I knew the lad,

And he was strong;
Or weak, or kind, or proud,
Or bold, or gay.
I knew him once.
But then he was a boy."
They ask me why I teach, and I reply,
"Where could I find more splendid company?"
—Author Unknown
—Wisconsin Education Journal

1277.   Teacher: "Did you fill out that blank?"
Student: "What blank?"
Teacher: "The blank between your ears."

1278.   We know a superintendent who doesn't hire cross-eyed teachers because they can't control their pupils.

1279.   A teacher affects eternity, he can never tell where his influence stops.

—Henry Brooks Adams

1280.   The children's program "Sesame Street," underwritten nationally by federal and foundation grants, has been widely praised for its extraordinary educational impact on youngsters.

One mother thought that her two-year-old son merely was being entertained until she discovered that he could repeat the alphabet, recognize all capital letters, count to 10 and recognize numerals.

"We had no idea he had learned so much so quickly," the mother said. "Now, if they would only include for these little geniuses a few segments on toilet training."

1281.   The secret of education lies in respecting the pupil.
—Ralph Waldo Emerson

1282.   It is the supreme art of the teacher to awaken joy in creative expression and knowledge.

—Albert Einstein

200

1283.   "I'm very sorry," the principal told his new teacher, "but if I let you take two hours off for lunch today and find a substitute for your class, I'd have to do the same for every other teacher whose wife gave birth to quadruplets."

1284.   It is essential that we enable young people to see themselves as participants in one of the most exciting eras in history, and to have a sense of purpose in relation to it.

—Rockefeller Report on Education

1285.   An elderly housemaster at Harrow School in England told a friend that as a young master, he had to cope with a most unruly class. In despair, he had exclaimed, "I don't know what to do with you boys," and a voice had answered him, "Please sir, teach us," the voice came from a chubby imp with carrot-colored hair—Winston Churchill.

1286.   A local school has gone in for team teaching. That's where the teachers gang up so no one can be held responsible.

—*Changing Times*

Teenagers (See High School, Students, Youth)

1287.   Parents, concerned about where their teenager is, might try following the telephone extension cord.

—*The Vandalie* (Ill.) *Union*

1288.   One way to keep teenagers out of hot water is to put dishes in it.

1289.   Teenagers today know *everything* . . . except the lessons the teacher assigned to them for tomorrow's class.

1290.   Rearing teenagers is like growing flowers. You have to keep weeding, hoeing, pinching back suckers and fertilizing. But you know if you do you will eventually have lovely blooms.

—Mrs. Christine C. Duenckel

1291.   To a teenager, social security is three dates for the same dance.

1292.   The main trouble with a teenager's transistor it's both AM and PM.

1293.   Everyone is disturbed these days. Teenagers are upset because they are living in a world dominated by nuclear weapons—and adults are upset because they're living in a world dominated by teenagers.

—Robert Orben

1294.   A stage is what many a teenage girl thinks she should be on, when actually it's just something she's going through.

1295.   Could it be that the reason rock-and-roll singers are so young is that if they were any older they'd be embarrassed?

1296.   Staring moodily out of his office window, a business tycoon reflected: "Ten thousand men jump to my slightest whim, but I can't persuade one teenage son to get a haircut."

1297.   The teenager played a new record favorite. Turning to her father, she exclaimed: "Oh-o-o, have you ever heard anything like it?"

He looked up and said: "Not really, dear. The closest thing to it I ever heard was when a truck loaded with empty cans ran into a truck full of hogs."

—Marsha Conner

1298.   Said one teenager: "You know, I'm starting to wonder what my parents were up to at my age that makes them so doggoned suspicious of me all the time!"

202

1299.   Too many parents tie up their dogs and let their 16-year-olds run loose.

1300.   The key to today's teenagers is often the one to the car.

1301.   "Who is that woman with Harry?" asked the wife.
"That's a distant relative," replied the husband. "It's his teenage daughter."

1302.   Classified ad: "For Sale. Complete set of encyclopedia. Never used. Teenage son knows everything."

1303.   A young teenager was going out on her first date with a new boyfriend.
"Are you sure this young fellow is a good driver?" asked the nervous father.
"Oh, yes," the girl replied. "He has to be. One more, and he'll lose his license."

1304.   Father: "I couldn't stand it any longer and finally washed all the make-up off my teenage daughter's face and pushed back all that hair, And do you know what? I've been bringing up somebody else's kid!"

1305.   A teenager doesn't always know where he's going; only that he isn't there.

1306.   It's hard for any teenager to realize that, in another 20 years, he will be as dumb as his parents are now.

1307.   One teenager said to another: "He hasn't actually kissed me yet, but he steamed my glasses a couple of times."

1308.   You'll notice it's the older fellows in the crowd who burn· their draft cards. The young ones need them when they try to buy beer.

1309.   Overheard at the office: "Now that I'm officially 18, I don't know whether to get married or go out and see an adult movie."

1310.   "Remember the good old days when you could see a teenager go into the garage and come out with a lawnmower?"

1311.   Teenage Mother: "Oh dear, I don't know what to do to make the baby stop crying?"
Teenage Father: "You've got to do something. Where's the book of instruction that came with the baby?"

1312.   If a four-year-old becomes uncontrollable and starts throwing things, it's called a temper tantrum. When a 20-year-old does it, it's called "a justified politically-oriented demonstration against the establishment."
—Smiles

1313.   When you watch teenagers dancing these days, you wonder what they do for relaxation.
—Smiles

1314.   If you ever wonder why the teenagers are like they are, watch a group of adults at a cocktail party sometime.
—William Branen in the *Burlington
Standard Press*

1315.   A modern teenager is a youngster who wants more out of life than there is in it.

1316.   To insure the education of teenagers, parents need to pull a few wires—television, telephone, and ignition.

1317.   Teenager writing home from boarding school: "Send food packages! All they serve here is breakfast, lunch and dinner."

1318. Teenagers aren't interested in putting their shoulders to the wheel. All they want is to get their hands on it.

Telephone

1319. The bathtub was invented in 1850 and the telephone in 1875. Had you been living in 1850, you could have sat in the bathtub for 25 years without the phone ringing once.

1320. Professor, calling wife to phone: "Dear, somebody wants to listen to you."

—Smiles

1321. An instructor and his family were having dinner when the phone rang. The youngest member was asked to answer it and said, "It sure is," and hung up. The same thing happened five minutes later.

"What's going on?" asked the father.

"Some crackpot keeps calling to say, 'it's long distance from New York.' " the youngster replied.

1322. Now that the telephone company has started to introduce television phones, we may get a lot of pleasure out of calling wrong numbers.

Television

1323. "Where is the English channel?" a teacher asked her class.

One of the "wiser" students blurted out: "I don't know. We can't get it on our set."

1324. They say that TV really is still in its infancy, which helps explain why you have to get up so much to change it.

1325. Television commercials are those brief moments students pay attention to their parents.

1326.   TV is remarkable. The same set that puts you to sleep, keeps your neighbors awake.

1327.   Student's seesickness is too much television.
—Farm Bureau News

1328.   We've finally found the educational channel on our TV set. It's marked "Off."
—Stan Ihenfeldt in the *Elkhorn Independent*

1329.   Young TV watchers will soon find out that the Man from Uncle is in reality the tax collector.

1330.   "I find TV very educational. Every time someone turns on the TV set, I go into the next room and read a book."
—Groucho Marx

1331.   Personally, I've always looked on daytime television as the punishment employers have come up with for workers who stay home when they're not really sick.

1332.   TV Announcer: "We have just received a bulletin about a catastrophe, the like of which has never been known to mankind—but first a word from our sponsor.

1333.   What this country needs is a good five-second commercial.

Theater (See Dramatics, Plays)

1334.   "Do you have many lines to speak in the new play?"
"No, I take the part of the husband."

1335.   An instructor and his wife were returning to their seats in the theater after the intermission.
"Did I step on your toes as I went out?" he asked a man at the end of the row.

"You did," replied the other grimly, expecting an apology.

The instructor turned to his wife and said: "All right, Mary. This is our row."

1336.   Usher: "How far down do you want to sit."
Patron: "All the way, of course."

1337.   The college producer was searching for new scenarios when one day in walked a new student with a manuscript under his arm.

"I understand you've got a new play," he said, leaning back in his chair. "Go ahead and read it to me."

The young author had not expected this treatment and was especially nonplussed because he had a terrible stammer since childhood. But the group was waiting so he sat down and read the whole script scene by scene.

"This is a great play," said the producer. "He's got a new twist that will have them rolling in the aisles. Every single character in his play stutters!"

1338.   Professor: "I've got tickets for the theater."
Wife: "Fine, I'll start dressing."
Professor: "Do that. The tickets are for tomorrow night."

Theory (See Science)

1339.   A "theory" is a hunch with a college education.

1340.   A medical journal advances the theory that "man is slightly taller in the morning than he is in the evening." We have never proved such a theory, but we have observed that we have a tendency to become "short" toward the end of the month.

Thought (See Education, Ideas)

1341.   Our best friends and our worst enemies are our thoughts. A thought can do us more good than a doctor or a banker or a faithful friend. It can also do us more harm than a brick.

1342.   When you stop to think, don't forget to start again.

—Voltaire

Time (See Age)

1343. Think wrongly, if you please; but in all cases think for yourself.

—Lessing

1344. Freethinkers are generally those who never think at all.

—Sterne

1345. There is nothing either good or bad, but thinking makes it so.

—Shakespeare

Time (See Age)

1346. To the June graduate whether from high school or college, these brief words from Emerson offer the best advice and guidance anyone could give: "Guard well your spare moments. They are like uncut diamonds. Discard them and their value will never be known; improve them and they will become the brightest gems in a useful life."

1347. A calendar is something that goes in one year and out the other.

1348. Time is a great healer but a poor beautician.

1349. Time is like a pipeful of tobacco. Pack it too tight and you can't draw anything good through it; fill it too loose and its fire goes dead.

1350. Time waits for no man—but it will stand still for a woman of 30.

1351. They say time is money, which makes us wonder why so many people waste it.

1352. Time is not an enemy unless you try to kill it.

1353.   People who have half an hour to spend usually spend it with someone who hasn't.

1354.   Time: the stuff between pay days.

1355.   Money lost can be replaced, but time lost is gone forever.

Tradition (See College, Schools)

1356.   The Dental Students Magazine says tradition is what schools get when they don't want to build new buildings.

1357.   Tradition is an important help to history, but its statements should be carefully scrutinized before we rely on them.

—Addison

1358.   Every tradition grows ever more venerable—the more remote is its origin, the more confused that origin is. The reverence due to it increases from generation to generation. The tradition finally becomes holy and inspires awe.

—Nietzsche

Traits (See Ability, Character)

1359.   Be yourself. Cultivate desirable qualities.
Be alert. Look for opportunities to express yourself.
Be positive. Determine your goal and the route to it.
Be systematic. Take one step at a time.
Be persistent. Hold to your course.
Be a worker. Work your brain more than your body.
Be a student. Know your job.
Be fair. Treat the other man as you would be treated.
Be temperate. Avoid excess in anything.
Be confident. Have faith that cannot be weakened.

—Dean Everett W. Lord

1360.   "Curiosity" makes people interesting and successful.

1361. Perseverance is the most overrated of traits if it is unaccompanied by talent. Beating your head against a wall is more likely to produce a concussion in the head than a hole in the wall.

—Sidney Harris in the *Chicago Daily News*

1362. Conceit is a queer disease. It makes everyone sick except the fellow who has it.

1363. Our only quarrel with an inferiority complex is that the people who need one never have it.

—Kiwanis Magazine

1364. Now that Spring has arrived, here's directions for Spring Planting:

First plant four rows of peas: Perseverance, presence, preparation, promptness.

Next plant three rows of Squash: Squash gossip, Squash criticism, Squash indifference.

Then add four rows of Lettuce: Let us be faithful to duty, Let us be unselfish and loyal, Let us be true to our obligations, Let us love one another.

No garden is complete without Turnips: Turn up for meetings, Turn up with a smile, Turn up with new ideas, Turn up with determination to make everything count for something good and worthwhile.

—Source Unkown

Tranquilizers (See Medicine, Drugs, Health)

1365. The mother of a problem child was advised by a psychiatrist: "You are far too upset and worried about your son. I suggest you take tranquilizers regularly."

On her next visit the psychiatrist asked: "Have the tranquilizers calmed you down?"

"Yes," the mother replied.

"And how is your son?" he asked

"Who cares," she replied.

1366. Professor: "So you have quit tranquilizers?"
Instructor: "I was forced to. I found myself being pleasant to people I wouldn't even speak to ordinarily."

1367. The "tranquilizer" is one of America's leading composers.

1368. Physician: "I advise you to take a tranquilizer before retiring."
Professor: "Before retiring? But won't I retire for another ten years."

Trust (See Character, Traits)

1369. A young student-couple sat in the Union at Arizona State University. I watched as the husband followed with his eyes a well-built coed who passed their table. Finally, his wife leaned over, patted his hand chidingly and said: "Don't trust anyone over 36-24-36."

—Clets Mundsack in *Readers' Digest*

1370. Can he be trusted? I should say not. He's so crooked that the wool he pulls over your eyes is half cotton.

Truth

1371. A three-year-old girl was asked by her pre-kindergarten teacher if she knew the meaning of the word, "truth."
"Truth," she said "is which one of us did it."

1372. It's not hard to find the truth. What is hard is not to run away from it once you have found it.

1373. I prefer credulity to skepticism, for there is more promise in almost anything than in nothing at all.

—R.B. Perry

1374. A lie is a poor substitute for truth, but is the only one that has been discovered.

1375. Some people have tact; others tell the truth.

V

Vacations (See Moonlighting, Students, Teachers)

1376. School opened and Junior lost his vacation job. His mother was paying him $1 a week not to play his drums.

1377. Ever notice how the rainy day for which you saved most generally comes during your vacation.

1378. Vacations would be wonderful if the wallet could take a rest too.

1379. The teacher was on vacation swimming in an unknown bay. He hollered to a man on shore: "Are you sure there are no crocodiles around here?"
"Absolutely," was the reply. "The sharks scare them away."

1380. How to spoil a Miami winter vacation: Cut Miami off northern weather information.

Valor (See Courage, Traits)

1381. Valor is to travel on an ocean liner without tipping. Discretion is to come back on a different ship.

Values (See Appreciation, Kindness, Love)

1382. It's good to have money and the things that money will buy, but it's good, too, to check up once in a while and make sure you haven't lost the things that money can't buy.

—G.H. Lorimer

1383. "To lose a friend is to die a little."

W

Weight and Diet (See Medicine)

1384. A college student who is about 25 pounds overweight, went to his physician for some reducing advice. The doctor wrote out a prescription and also gave him a bottle of little blue pills.

"These are not to be swallowed," he directed the student. "Spill them on the floor of your dormitory room several times a day and then pick them up."

1385. It's not hard to diet when you're going to college. Just eat what you can afford.

1386. The instructor says that his wife sees to it that they have a balanced diet. The food bill always equals his pay.

1387. There's a reducing salon on the campus that offers satisfaction guaranteed or double your tummy back.

1388. Have you noticed when you go on a diet the first thing you lose is your temper?

1389. A sure fire diet is one where you never eat while your wife is talking.

1390. Campus Doctor: "Follow this diet, Miss Jones, and in two months I want to see three-fourths of you back here for a check-up."

Wisdom (See Ability, Education, Genius)

1391. Wisdom comes with age—too late to do any good.

1392. Common sense, in an uncommon degree, is what the world calls wisdom.

—Coleridge

1393. A wise woman puts a grain of sugar into everything she says to a man and takes everything he says to her with a grain of salt.

1394. Another argument for keeping one's mouth shut is that it is easier to look wise than to speak wisely.

1395. Full strength wisdom comes when we face up to the fact that we are no longer indispensable.

1396. The growth of wisdom may be gauged accurately by the decline of ill temper.

—Nietzsche

1397. An optimist is a person who sees green light everywhere while the pessimist sees only the red stop light... But the truly wise person is color-blind.

—Albert Schweitzer

1398. It is easy to be witty and wicked and hard to be witty and wise.

—Marie Rasey

Words (See English, Grammar, Spelling)

1399. The teacher was trying to explain the meaning of certain words to her class. She came to the word "Sufficient."

"Now," she said, "Suppose there was a cat here and I gave it a saucer of milk which it drank. Then I gave it another saucerful and it drank it all. But when I gave it a third, it would drink only half of it. We can then say the cat had sufficient. Now then, Richard, what is the meaning of "sufficient?"

"A cat full of milk," Richard answered eagerly.

1400. The teacher had impressed on her pupils the importance of knowing the meaning of new words. At home that night, Sharon heard the word "extinct" on a television program and asked grandmother what it meant.

"Well, it's like this," the grandmother replied, "if all the people in the world disappeared, you could say the human race is extinct."

Sharon thought a minute and then asked, "But who would I say it to?"

1401.   Synonym: "A word you use when you can't spell the word you thought of first."

1402.   Teacher to Kenneth: "Kenneth, what is an awl?"
Kenneth: "A southern owl."

1403.   A man with a good vocabulary is one who can describe a shapely woman without using his hands.

1404.   What a relief! The New American College Dictionary authorizes us to pronounce "vase" either way.

1405.   The average woman's vocabulary is about 1,000 words—small inventory but large turnover.

1406.   A smart man can do almost anything if he uses the right words on the right listeners. A classic example was during a senatorial election campaign in back-country Florida, when one candidate told his audience these facts about his opponent:

"You ought to know," he said, "That Senator Turbid is known all over Washington as a shameless extrovert. Not only that, but this man practices nepotism with his sister-in-law and he has a sister who was once a thespian in New York City. Worst of all, before his marriage, Senator Turbid habitually practiced celibacy."

1407.   The Lord's Prayer contains 56 words; Lincoln's Gettysburg address, 260; the Ten Commandments, 300; the Declaration of Independence, 3,000; a recent government order setting the price of cabbage, 26,911.

1408.   "Gee," said the admiring schoolboy, "where did you pick up that good bad word?"

—Lane Olinghouse

1409. When you feel exhilarated, but can't pronounce it, you've had enough to drink.

1410. The man who eats his own words won't ask for seconds.

1411. The following story is particulary useful in illustrating clarity in writing and verbose language.

It concerns a plumber who was having problems clearing plumbing drains and thought he had found a new effective method with the use of Hydrochloric Acid.

He began to wonder, however, if the acid might hurt the drains so he wrote the U.S. Government Bureau of Standards and asked them to advise him about the use of Hydrochloric Acid in cleaning drains.

The Bureau Answered:

"The efficiency of Hydrochloric Acid is indisputable, but the corrosive residue is incompatible with metallic permanence."

A few weeks went by and the plumber wrote another letter thanking the Bureau for approving his new method.

The bureau, worried, wrote again—this time more emphatically.

"We cannot assume responsibility for the production of toxic and noxious residue with Hydrochloric Acid and suggest that you use an alternate method."

A month went by and the plumber wrote another letter:

"Yep," he wrote, "the acid was working just fine and he couldn't thank the Bureau enough for recommending it to him."

This time the Bureau did what it should have done in the first place. It wrote:

"Quit using Hydrochloric Acid. It eats the Hell out of pipes!"

Worry

1412. Worry kills more people than work, they say. That figures. More people worry than work.

1413. Worry is like a rocking chair. It will give you something to do but won't get you anywhere.

1414. Worry whittles more precious hours out of our days and lops more years off our lives than we can measure. Why do we let worry browbeat us so much? Bertrand Russell once wrote that we can get the upper hand over worry just by out-thinking it: "Worry is a form of fear, and all forms of fear produce fatigue. A man who has learned not to fear will find the fatigue of daily life enormously diminished... Every form of fear grows worse by not being looked at. ... The proper course with every kind of fear is to think about it rationally and calmly, but with great concentration, until it has become completely familiar. In the end familiarity will blunt its terrors."

In other words, worry won't be there unless we suffer it to remain. A worry is a magnification of whatever threat really exists. As Mark Twain once said: "I am an old man and have known a great many troubles, but most of them never happened."

—Nuggets

Writing (See English, Journalism, Language, Literature, Spelling, Words)

1415.   Teacher: "Paul, why are you writing with such large letters?"

Paul: "I'm writing to my grandmother. She's deaf, so I have to write loud for her!"

—Trux

1416.   A good writer fills his own wastebasket rather than his reader's.

—H.J. Tichy

1417.   Charles Lamb, of Plagiarism, said: "It is true I milked twenty cows to get the milk, but so help me, the butter I churned is all mine."

1418.   The following is credited to the English author, Hilair Belloc:

"When I am dead, I hope it may be said! 'His sins were scarlet, but his books were read.' "

1419.   A woman on television, participating in a show, was asked the name of her favorite author. "Why, it's my husband," she replied.

"Your husband?" questioned the interviewer. "And what does he write?"

The woman smiled brightly, "Checks."

Youth (See Adolescence, Teenagers, Students)

1420.   The bigger the author the smaller the words he uses.

Y

Youth (See Adolescence, Teenagers, Students)

1421.   Youth is when we are looking for greener fields and middle age is when we can hardly mow the one we've got.
>   —Margaret Lee in the *Deerfield Independent*

1422.   Today's youth is more sophisticated. If Booth Tarkington were to write Seventeen today, he would have to call it Twelve.

1423.   To stay youthful, stay useful.
>   —*Construction Digest*

1424.   Youth having its fling is not so bad, but we do object to some of the things they're throwing.

1425.   Today's youth no longer have to run away from home— they drive.

1426.   In the old days a boy would give his girl his class ring when they were going steady. Nowadays he lets her use his hair curlers.

1427.   You're only a youth once. After that it takes another excuse.

Z

Zoology (See Animals, Biology)

1428.   While visiting the zoo with her class, a youngster saw her first peacock. "Look teacher," she said, "there's a living color."

INDEX

Index